LOUISE WREN

The Little
Red Thief

THE TRUE STORY OF

FOXYLOXY

AN ORPHANED FOX CUB

LOUISE WREN

The Little
Red Thief

THE TRUE STORY OF
FOXYLOXY
AN ORPHANED FOX CUB

MEREO
Cirencester

Mereo Books

1A The Wool Market Dyer Street Cirencester Gloucestershire GL7 2PR
An imprint of Memoirs Publishing www.mereobooks.com

The Little Red Thief: 978-1-86151-181-2

First published in Great Britain in 2014
by Mereo Books, an imprint of Memoirs Publishing

The address for Memoirs Publishing Group Limited can be found at
www.memoirspublishing.com

Cover design - Ray Lipscombe

The Memoirs Publishing Group Ltd Reg. No. 7834348

The Memoirs Publishing Group supports both The Forest Stewardship Council® (FSC®) and
the PEFC® leading international forest-certification organisations. Our books carrying both the
FSC label and the PEFC® and are printed on FSC®-certified paper. FSC® is the only
forest-certification scheme supported by the leading environmental organisations including
Greenpeace. Our paper procurement policy can be found at
www.memoirspublishing.com/environment

Typeset in 11.5/15pt Goudy
by Wiltshire Associates Publisher Services Ltd. Printed and bound in Great Britain by
Printondemand-Worldwide, Peterborough PE2 6XD

Contents

For my family, friends and all animal lovers,
with special love to Emma and Marcus.

Foreword

Foxes in the UK tend to suffer a very bad press. By sharing my experience and telling this story, I am hoping to dispel some of the myths that surround foxes and to show that, contrary to the popular belief that foxes are dirty, aggressive vermin, they are beautiful, graceful and sentient wild animals with a family life just like you and me.

I knew absolutely nothing about foxes before Foxyloxy turned up in my garden and want the reader to know that it was entirely her decision to be my friend and that, at all times, she was a wild urban fox, free to come and go as she wished.

I was very privileged that Foxyloxy chose to trust me. She changed my life.

CHAPTER ONE

A fox cub in the garden

'Hello little foxy, what are you doing there? Aren't you beautiful!'

These were the first words I ever spoke to a fox. That in itself was no strange occurrence; I adore all animals, so it was quite normal for me to speak to one. But, as they are so shy and wary of humans, I had never spoken to a fox - until now, they had never come near enough.

It was the end of May 2011 and I was upstairs in my house looking out of my bedroom window, before closing it for the night and drawing the curtains, when I was very surprised to see a fox cub sitting on my front lawn. It seemed very small and it looked up at me when I spoke to it. I could see it quite clearly; it was a lovely little animal. Imagine my surprise when it did not run away immediately when it spotted me. I was delighted; it was a stunning, perfect little fox.

Seldom had I seen one so small – or so near - and I wondered where its mother was. It just sat quite still with its tail neatly curled around its feet, looking up at me and listening to my voice; I talked to it some more, but eventually it lost interest and sauntered off down the road.

Thus began a very special relationship, one which lasted well over a year and changed my perception of foxes forever. It also changed me in a way I could not have imagined. As I learned more and more about these animals, I became increasingly protective of them. In the process, I gained many new friends.

Foxes in our road and gardens had been a regular occurrence. I have lived in the same house in suburban Surrey for 48 years and there have always been foxes around. Over the years I had seen them in the distance, and in the autumn I had heard their blood-curdling screaming and barking, which made me think a murder was being committed. I even phoned 999 on one occasion. When I was told the noise was being made by foxes, I could hardly believe it. I cringe now to think of it. How could I, an animal lover, have been so ignorant? I guess bringing up a family while studying and working full-time had got in the way of learning more about animals.

Occasionally, when working in the front garden, I saw a fox strolling by in broad daylight. There was other evidence of foxes as well; shoes and gardening gloves disappeared mysteriously off the doorsteps in the cul-de-sac where I live, and I found the occasional smelly scat, or flattened flowers and branches broken off the shrubs and plants in the garden. Once I even found a beheaded duck on the back door step; at the time, I blamed my cat and wondered how he had managed to drag something that big back from the little stream on the corner of the road.

In addition to all these signs, foxes have a very

distinctive smell. They mark their territories by scenting and urinating, which tells other foxes they are there – there is absolutely no mistaking 'Eau de Reynard'.

I had also seen foxes running about in the road at night, and sometimes I had watched them playing with a ball left outside by the children who live here in the small cul-de-sac. I thought foxes were quite delightful, and I watched them with fascination whenever I saw them - the way they wagged their tails and played with the ball and each other. The way they were taking turns in picking up the ball, throwing it about and chasing it reminded me of puppies. I certainly did not mind them being around and was always intrigued by them and thrilled to see them. Apart from a bit of noise, they did not seem to be doing anybody any harm. Little did I know then that one day I would become a huge fox fan, and that their presence would so enrich my life. One fox in particular did this, and that was Foxyloxy.

Before I first saw 'my' cub sitting in the front garden, I had quite often heard snuffling, scratching and squabbling noises in the border under the bedroom window for a few weeks. I am a light sleeper, so the unusual sounds had woken me up immediately. Looking out of the bedroom window to see what could be the source of this noise, I saw a big fox and two cubs running about on the grass and in the borders under the front window. Never having seen little fox cubs before, I watched in fascination as they rummaged around in the grass and among the shrubs, with the vixen watching them closely. The cubs were like miniature versions of the vixen; they looked like toys. She was obviously their mother; they stayed close by her and she watched them, groomed them, and suckled them. It was touching to see how caring she was.

I now know they must have been about 7-8 weeks old at the time, because that is approximately the age when cubs come out of the den and start to follow their mum around at night. They were rummaging for earthworms, grubs, beetles and other foxy delicacies, maybe hoping to catch a mouse even. In addition, there were always peanuts and dog biscuits on the lawn at night, and I will tell you why.

The previous autumn I had found a pair of my leather gardening shoes, which I had left on the back doorstep, in another part of the back garden – both shoes thoroughly chewed up. At the time, I was confused; had somebody been in my garden? Could my cats have done such damage to the shoes? It seemed unlikely; whole chunks of the leather were missing. I know they are a pair of greedy tabbies but surely they had not eaten it. The next pair of shoes I left at the back door met the same fate a few weeks later. How odd!

It was a mystery, but I finally concluded that it must have been a fox and I thought that maybe it chewed the shoes because it was hungry. After all, I had always heard that 'foxes eat anything'. I decided to test my theory and left a couple of sausages out on the patio that night; they disappeared before I went to bed. The next night, pieces of cheese and some quiche also vanished; the night after that, as I had no other leftovers, I made a ham sandwich, which was gone 15 minutes after I put it outside. I did feel a bit of a fool, making a sandwich for a possibly imaginary fox, but nobody knew. However, I could not be sure that it was not one of the neighbourhood cats eating the food. About 12 of the 19 families in the Close owned cats at that time and although my own cats are always indoors with me at night, there are many others out-and-about in this road at night.

However, I began to suspect that I did have a nightly foxy visitor in my back garden.

Being a natural 'nurturer', I could not bear to think of any creature going hungry, so I bought some cheap dog biscuits and put them in a bowl. I reasoned with myself that a cat would not eat dog biscuits, fussy eaters that they are. I still had no positive proof though. One night, my own two cats alerted me to the presence of something in the back garden; their ears pricked up and even though they appeared fast asleep next to me on the sofa, they suddenly jumped up and rushed over to the patio doors to look out.

By the way, how do cats do that? When I call mine, they don't hear me, yet if another animal is strolling quietly around in their garden they hear it immediately - even when they are sleeping.

The next night it happened again, and this time I was hot on their furry heels. I peered carefully around the curtain and I saw a small fox right there on my patio eating the dog biscuits; it immediately ran away when it saw me looking. However, I had the proof I needed.

Now that I was sure of my visitor, I left a little bit of food out every night that autumn and all through the winter. I would find the bowl empty every morning. Although I did not see much of the fox, I like to think I was helping a wild animal survive the winter. After all, I fed all the birds and squirrels in the garden and provided water as well.

The *Springwatch* programme on TV showed both badgers and foxes eating peanuts, so in May, I started to sprinkle a mixture of dog biscuits and peanuts on the front lawn where I now heard the foxes in the night. I concluded that the fox I had seen at night on the lawn must have been a vixen which had led her cubs to a source of food, and that was why they were foraging on my lawn and in the borders. This solved the mystery of the nocturnal noises.

I was thrilled with my foxy visitors and watched them many a night; I wondered - could this be the same fox I had been feeding all winter?

Their appearance in my garden was a regular nocturnal occurrence until around early June, when suddenly the vixen and one of the cubs stopped coming. I never saw either of them again, but the second little cub was now sitting on my lawn, looking at me. I wondered if it had become an orphan at that young age. The reason I thought this was that around this time I saw a dead vixen with a cub close by her at the side of the main road, about half a mile from my house. It looked as if a car had hit them and they had died together as they had tried to cross the road; a tragic discovery, which made me feel very sad.

Not far from my road is a railway embankment on the other side of the main road, where I had sometimes seen foxes. The animals would have to cross this road in order to get into our estate on this side. I had occasionally seen fox casualties on this road and I wondered if this latest pair of bodies could have been the mother and sibling of the fox cub that was presently sitting on my lawn all alone, as it seemed too much of a coincidence. I felt desperately sorry for it, as it looked too small to be without its mother.

It was now early June, so it cannot have been more than three or four months old. Most cubs are born from the end of February onwards, although some can be born as late as the beginning of April. It all depends on when the adults mated - usually in late December or January.

The fox population in the UK remains fairly stable. Research has shown that approximately fifty per cent of all fox cubs will never make it to the autumn; many more foxes will never even get through the winter because of cold, starvation, disease, accidents, poisoning or fighting. In addition, if a vixen dies in the early days of the cubs' life, the entire litter is in danger of starvation as they cannot fend for themselves and cannot eat solid foods.

Fox cubs are very playful and inquisitive and while exploring can sometimes become trapped in garden netting, fencing and wiring. Some drown in ponds and even in swimming pools. However, the majority of fox casualties come from road accidents. Each year, many adult foxes and cubs become victims, especially in the spring when vixens travel further afield to search for food for their cubs, and in the autumn when family units break up and inexperienced youngsters start to disperse to look for new territories at the end of the summer. I am not going to mention the number of foxes killed by farmers, gamekeepers and hunters, it upsets me too much. Foxes only have one litter of four or five cubs in the spring, which compensates for the loss of adults and cubs each year; the life span of an urban fox is approximately two years, although a captive one can live as long as 14 years.

Getting to know Foxyloxy

The little fox I had seen on the lawn now continued coming to the garden on its own every night and was eating the dog biscuits and peanuts. Shortly afterwards, during the school half term break, my two grandchildren, Emma (13) and Marcus (10), came to stay. They live 75 miles away on the south coast and it has always been easier for them to come and move in with me during school holidays when their parents are both working.

They have been coming since they were very small and, among other outings, the three of us have had a lovely time exploring the Surrey countryside, watching and identifying the garden birds, going on bat walks, nature trails, pond dipping, shelter-building expeditions, wildlife spotting and other nature-related activities. I am lucky to I live in a very beautiful part of Surrey and I loved the fact that the children seemed as interested in nature as I was when I was a girl.

I have my aunt and uncle to thank for that; I spent a lot of time with them and, from an early age, they always took me walking in the dunes and woods in Holland, where I grew up. I loved going to children's farms and zoos to see the animals. My uncle knew the names of all the wildlife we spotted, and my aunt taught me the Latin names of all the flowers and plants in her garden. Somehow I remembered all these, and I still do.

I began passing on this knowledge to my grandchildren and before long, they knew the names of all the birds visiting in my garden, such as blackbirds, dunnocks, robins, blue tits, great tits, wagtails, jays, magpies, nuthatches, collared doves and a variety of pigeons, to name but a few. We took photographs and fed them all and when we did not know what kind of bird it was, we looked it up in my wildlife book, so we were learning together. We visited wildlife parks and sanctuaries, such as the Highland Wildlife Park with its wolves and reindeer and the Osprey Centre, both near Aviemore in Scotland. The Hawk Conservancy Centre near Andover with its flying displays always proved a big hit, as did the Otter Sanctuary in Cornwall.

Nearer home, we visited children's farms, where we handled animals. We adopted a donkey at a rescue centre for donkeys and ponies, walked with llamas, watched flying displays and fed ducks, swans and geese on the local lakes and ponds. Nature walks around my area always included a 'who can spot the most interesting wildlife' game. We sometimes saw pheasants, a deer or rabbits, but never a fox. Still, it was all good fun.

I put feeders in the garden and we had fun making charts to see how many of each species of bird visited. There was always something going on outside. The squirrels were especially amusing to watch with their antics: swinging on the feeders, using the washing line as a high wire and stealing the chocolate Easter eggs hidden in the garden. So when I told the children that I had a visiting fox cub in the garden, they were very excited. Never having seen a fox in real life before, they could not wait to see it.

During the half term week they were here in June, they spent ages at night watching from the bedroom windows to see if they could spot the fox. Keeping quiet and not moving the curtain too much was such a challenge for them at first, as the little fox would run away as soon as she spotted us. I devised a cunning plan: every night when it was time for bed, we would do a 'Fox Watch'. I had noticed that the fox would always appear shortly after I had put the food out. This Fox Watch involved the children getting ready for bed, me putting some food out and then all of us waiting eagerly at the upstairs windows for an appearance. She fascinated them as much as she fascinated me. In June, it was not all that dark at the time she appeared and we had a great view of the front garden and the road from the bedroom windows upstairs.

We speculated whether our fox was a boy or a girl; then, seeing her squatting on the lawn one night to urinate I decided it was probably a girl; the children named her 'Foxyloxy', and Foxyloxy she remained.

Sometimes, other foxes appeared as well and furious fights over food ensued. I once saw three foxes having a tug-of-war with the food bowl; however, our little one stood her ground. She snarled and chased the bigger ones away like a good 'un. It was her territory and her mother's territory before her and she would not back off - good for her.

Now that she had a name, I would call her by name when I put her bowl of food out at night - 'Foxyloxy, dinner time!' Without fail, she would appear shortly after that. She came from the direction of the woodland path that connects the Close with the main road, setting off a few security lights on her way to my house, so I always knew she was on her way. She did not seem to live too far away, and we soon became hooked on watching her. I carried on the ritual of calling Foxyloxy, leaving her food and then watching her, even when the children went back home. Most of the time, she seemed to be by herself. I was fascinated by her.

Six weeks after that visit, at the end of July, Emma and Marcus were back to stay for the summer holiday. They were very keen to see the fox again and resumed their watching activities from the bedroom windows during the evenings. It was always a great way to get them to go upstairs at night! Foxes were not the only creatures we watched out for: at dusk, we could also see Pipistrelle bats flying around the trees. The children thought this was a very exciting house with all the different types of wildlife around.

One night, despite the cool, damp summer, they wanted to 'camp' in the back garden – as children do. 'You do realise Foxyloxy may come into the garden and visit you', I warned them. 'We are not worried about that', was the reply. I do believe they were hoping she would. Together we erected the tent in the back garden, the cushions from the sun loungers serving as mattresses, and then we dragged sheets, pillows and duvets down from the beds upstairs. Naturally, their teddy bears would also camp out. With solar lights repositioned to point the way to the back door, which would remain unlocked for them, the garden gate locked, the outside light on, and a torch each they were going to be safe and warm. Even my nosey cats soon settled in the tent with them!

Suddenly, I spotted the back gate was still open... safe, indeed! As I went to lock it, a movement near the front door startled me. It turned out to be Foxyloxy and, as usual, she was waiting for her food - I had not even had the time to call her. I told the children the fox was by the front door. All thoughts of sleeping vanished as they immediately got up, ran out of the tent and shone their torches in her direction. 'Oh no', I warned, 'you will frighten her!'

However, instead of being frightened off and running away, she just stood there and watched us. She cannot have been more than 16 feet or so away. We tried to keep as quiet as possible and I went inside to get her food. Emma ran in to get the camera in order to take her picture. 'Oh no, don't', I said again, 'you will scare her off'. Not listening to me, Emma took some pictures, with the flash even, which Foxyloxy did not seem to mind at all, much to my surprise.

It was so thrilling to watch her that close to us; we were downstairs and outside instead of upstairs looking at her from the bedroom window. We were so excited! I put her food down by the side of the house and slowly backed away; she came a little bit closer and started eating, keeping a wary eye on us, while two very excited children and I admired her from a distance. She was just beautiful, with a lovely red bushy tail ending in a tiny white tip and a delicate, sweet face with golden eyes that glowed in the light of the torches. She seemed very small for a five-month-old cub, not that I then had any idea how big they should be.

Marcus whispered 'I wish I could cuddle her'. How sweet! I knew how he felt but explained that she was a wild animal and that we could never touch her, as she would not like that and might feel threatened and scared. After taking photos, we left her to eat in peace and when she finished and walked away, I locked the gate. It had been a most exciting fox watch. The photos turned out rubbish, by the way, which was a little disappointing.

The next evening, I went upstairs to close the curtains when I noticed Foxyloxy curled up on the front lawn, close to the house. She was watching the house and it was still quite light. She looked just like a little dog, all curled up with her tail wrapped around her covering her nose. I ran down the stairs and said, 'You are not going to believe this! Foxyloxy is lying on the lawn waiting for us'. It turned out that this was exactly what she was doing - she was there waiting for her dinner and, once again, I had not called her. Amazing!

This time we carefully opened the front door and put her bowl on the path nearby. She looked wary, stood up and backed off to the road, so we closed the door again and watched her eat from the window downstairs, which she did not seem to mind.

For the next two weeks, we had a new bedtime routine: we looked out for her downstairs; every night she sat on the lawn around the same time and we gave her some food by the front door. Her food consisted of dog biscuits and peanuts with a few bits of chicken or other leftovers on top. I also put a dish with clean water outside. Slowly she came closer as we moved the bowl a few inches nearer to us every night. She finally felt brave enough to eat under the porch while we watched her quietly from the hall with the door open.

It was an excellent opportunity to study her more closely and photograph her. She did not mind the camera in the least, nor the flash, nor even our excited giggling and whispering. Little did I know then that she would turn out to be a natural poser and supermodel. We were just amazed, and watched in wonder as she ate her food. This beautiful wild animal had come to trust us not to hurt her. Nothing could have been further from our minds in any case.

There were some occasions however, when she would not come close to us, and we soon found out why. She appeared to be afraid of cats, which was news to me; I had always thought that it was the other way around. But when there was a cat near our house, or when one of my cats was in the hall she kept a safe distance between her and the cat. So odd, she was wild and much bigger than the cats, yet she was very wary. I had always thought foxes would chase cats. It would appear I was wrong. Mind you, foxes sometimes attack a nosey cat who tries to get into a den with squealing cubs, in which case she would just be defending her babies, like most animal mothers; the cat would have killed the tiny cubs, mistaking them for rats perhaps.

Later I would learn that foxes are very wary of fighting with cats, the main reason being that cats have better weaponry: a fox's teeth versus the teeth *and* 16 sharp claws of a cat. No competition, so best avoid a confrontation, eh foxy?

Learning about foxes

One day, the children and I went on a visit to the British Wildlife Centre in Surrey. There, among many other species of wildlife, we saw rescued foxes, which they were unable to release back into the wild for one reason or another. We watched in stunned silence as a vixen named Honey came up to the keeper and took food from his hand while her grown-up cub, Buster, who was more fearful, kept hiding in the shrubs. There were five foxes in the enclosure altogether; Honey was the only one who came close to the keeper and took food from his hand. We were amazed to see this close-up encounter and we wondered if our fox would do that. Wouldn't that be something! I have to mention here that, at that time, I didn't know you should never feed a wild fox by hand; I didn't really know anything about foxes and it looked so much fun. But then, Honey was a captive fox.

We saw many species of wild animal that day at this wonderful centre, but we had especially enjoyed seeing the foxes and the badgers. We couldn't get enough of them and during the journey back home, I had two children in animal masks in the car, a 'Vulpes vulpes' and a 'Meles meles', the Latin names for the red fox and the badger respectively. The children liked the Latin names and they remember them to this day.

On another morning, we had to make an emergency trip to the Wildlife Hospital in Leatherhead. The day before, Marcus had found a wood pigeon that was unable to fly. He was walking the dog with my friend and had seen it come crashing through the trees along the woodland lane after other pigeons had chased it; he had run home to tell me, as he did not know how to pick it up. Emma, who wants to be a vet, went to collect it armed with a tea towel and a shoebox, and brought it back home. I could not see any obvious injury apart from the fact that the left wing was hanging down a little. We put the bird in the cat's carrier basket, with some water and birdseed, and covered it with a towel to keep it dark and quiet as I thought it might just be shocked. We phoned the local Wildlife Hospital for advice; they asked us to keep it overnight and to try to see if it could fly the next morning after a good rest, so we left it in peace in a cool place.

The pigeon looked fine the next morning. We all had a good look at it as I held it; the colours and patterns of its feathers were amazing in close up. They are much more beautiful than you would think, with colours in their shimmering plumage varying from grey, brown, black and mauve to white and shades thereof. I thought it held its wing better, so I put it on top of the bird table and stood back. It tried to fly away, but almost immediately fell to the ground again. We were devastated; I picked the bird up from the lawn and phoned the hospital again to say we were bringing it in.

Off to Leatherhead we went, where we checked the pigeon in for an examination. While we waited, we wandered out and noticed foxes in the outside pens. They all had an injury of some description and some even had a leg in a blue plaster cast. In order to be able to return foxes to the wild after treatment the hospital staff minimise human contact, so we only had a sneaky peek at them; we thought they looked very sad in their pens, so different from the lovely girl we knew at home. It was obvious that these foxes were not happy to be in hospital and would rather have been in their natural environment.

Staff told us that they would recover soon and the hospital would release them again, and always in the area where they had been found. Foxes use their long, slim front legs for hunting and digging, so a broken front leg is obviously a disaster, although a broken back leg usually heals by itself, leaving the fox with no more than a limp. It was all news to us.

Our pigeon however was not so lucky; after the vet had examined it the nurse told us that they could do nothing for it and that euthanasia was the only option. They could not repair the badly-broken wing and 'she', as she turned out to be, would never be able to fly again. Poor 'Penny' pigeon - oh yes, Marcus had named her. We were shocked, it was terrible news and the children cried in the car all the way home. I joined in; we are all very soft about nature's creatures. What a dreadful day. We needed a sweet fix to recover from the shock, so after we got home we had drinks and chocolate biscuits all round. Phew, what an experience!

Later that year, the three of us went on holidays to Spain. While there, we visited the private Lobo Wolf Park in Andalusia. The park is huge and has only been open to the public since 2004. The wolf pups are all born there and are not domesticated, just socialised by bottle-feeding them for a while when they are born; later nobody touches them or interferes with them, and they are never hand-fed. This makes it possible for visitors to observe their truly wild behaviour and study them closely. The aim of the park owner is to educate people. Since wolves are very timid animals, it would be almost impossible to observe the animals in their natural habitat otherwise. In this park, they live as naturally as possible in very large enclosures in beautiful, natural woodland surroundings, and all have access to freshwater ponds.

It was a fantastic day out. Among all the different varieties of wolf, we saw the one and only white wolf left in Europe, which was quite sad.

Besides the wolves, there were a number of other rescued animals, including a few foxes. Ah, foxes again! One in particular, Oscar, melted our hearts when he just snuggled up into the keeper's arms and enjoyed a tummy rub and a cuddle. We learned that he had come to the park after a car accident; the park was unable to release him back into the wild because of brain damage, so he was a permanent resident. As soon as the keeper went into the foxes' pen, Oscar jumped up into her arms. Well, if foxes could purr, Oscar would have done so. His delight was obvious; we all saw it in the way he was lying back in his keeper's arms, belly up, with his feet in the air, tail gently wagging and his eyes closed in ecstasy. The keeper informed us he would have stayed there all day if she had let him!

On our return home from Spain, Foxyloxy was waiting for us. Every night during our absence, my neighbour, Jenny, had fed her at my house so that she would not be without food; she had only caught a glimpse of her once. However, the minute we were back and called her, Foxyloxy appeared. It was endearing to think she knew us, and we were delighted to see her.

All these foxy encounters had heightened our perception of foxes and we were now very eager to learn more about them. One rainy day we attended the local RSPCA Gala Day, where we met a member of Surrey Wildlife Trust, told him about our Foxyloxy, and showed him her photograph. I was getting a little worried about feeding her and was worried that she might possibly not know how to teach her cubs how to hunt for themselves - should she have some in due course. He put my mind at rest and said that she would not lose her instinct and that the cubs would be completely wild.

He also gave me a small booklet about foxes. It was a little guide called 'Fox UK' written by Professor Stephen Harris, a zoologist and an expert on foxes. As well as the invaluable advice and information in the booklet, it contained anecdotes and photographs from other people who had experienced foxy encounters and visitors to their gardens. I loved seeing the photos and reading the little stories; it seemed we were not the only ones pleased to see them.

In the back of the booklet was list of groups and charities who offer news and advice on the welfare of foxes. Furthermore, it included a list of foods that foxes would eat. I read it from cover to cover and started to supplement Foxyloxy's diet with leftovers from our dinner, scraps of meat and pieces of chicken, including the carcass, and an occasional apple or pear. She grew bigger and more beautiful every week, she looked glorious!

Keen to find out as much as I could about foxes, I searched the internet and learned even more about them. Unfortunately, I also found out how much some people hate them and actually consider them vermin. 'Vermin' they are not. They are just beautiful wild animals that will actually eat rats and mice, which are truly vermin. I was horrified to read stories of trapping, snaring, poisoning and hunting, which seemed so cruel. Our towns and cities have expanded and humans have built on land where foxes once lived and hunted.

Being intelligent and highly opportunistic, foxes have made the most of this by learning to forage for food left by us wasteful and untidy humans. Far from scavenging desperately for scraps because they cannot find food elsewhere, urban foxes are taking full advantage of the tasty larder we have created on their doorstep, from half-finished take-away meals to bags of rubbish left out for the refuse collectors. And of course, they have taken full advantage of our own interest in them and our desire to care for them – as in my case. Meanwhile rural foxes continue to live as they have always lived, hunting for wild animals, birds, eggs and any other form of protein they can find - and occasionally raiding hen runs, which is one reason why country people generally are not so indulgent as we 'townies'!

Many people have of course been devastated to find that their chickens, pet rabbits or guinea pigs have been killed by a fox. Naturally it is the owner's responsibility to keep their livestock and pets safe. Foxes are very intelligent and can easily undo a simple twisting lock.

There seemed to be plenty of information available on these lovely animals, and they were definitely not the vicious killers that some people believe them to be. Opportunistic, yes, but as I read about them and watched videos clips of them playing with cats and even dogs it showed me they were not natural killers. After all, when a dog or cat feels threatened it will also defend itself and might bite you.

When you find a fox in your home, it tends to be there because it is ill and seeks shelter. Unless you have a piece of meat lying on the kitchen table and have left the door open of course. Mind you, a dog would steal that as well, if it got the chance, and my cats are not beyond stealing some tuna if I leave it on the worktop unattended.

I asked my friend across the road whether he had ever lost a rabbit – he has three rabbits in his garden in a nice hutch with bolts and a large attached outside run. He told me he had once lost one rabbit to a fox – years ago. 'I learned my lesson' he said. He dug down a foot or so to put the protective chicken wire edges of the run into the ground, then put concrete slabs on top of the soil all along the outside edge of the run. There was no way a fox could dig underneath the run to get in, and they had never done it again. Oh yes, he had seen foxes in the garden since, but had never experienced any more problems. They just sat and watched his rabbits occasionally.

On the other hand, another of my neighbours lost a couple of guinea pigs, one to a cat and one to a fox. He used to let them run around his garden without any supervision, so who was to blame there? I felt sure it was not the fox. All owners of poultry and pets such as rabbits and guinea pigs should protect them securely. Why blame the fox for getting an easy meal when it is just following nature? I found many tips on the internet on how to make a cage or run fox-proof.

When a fox gets into a poultry enclosure it will often appear to go on the rampage, attacking every hen it can reach and leaving a trail of dead and dying birds. This is cited as evidence of the fox's cruel and bloodthirsty nature, even that it kills for fun, but it is simply taking advantage of a rare opportunity to take a large quantity of food. By artificially cooping up a large quantity of prey creatures in a confined space, we are setting the scene for a massacre. If a fox can find a way into the enclosure it will kill all the hens it can and take away what it can carry, caching the birds, usually by burying them, and come back for more later on to feed itself and its family.

Though the fox doesn't see it this way, it is a bit like us going to the supermarket – we usually do not go to buy food for just one meal, we buy for several meals and 'stash' it in the fridge to eat later or to feed our family. We eat because we are hungry and we need to feed our children, and foxes are no different. However, there is one huge difference; foxes do not hunt, inflict pain or kill for fun… need I say more? I find it distressing when I read in the press how they are vilified and what people believe about foxes as a consequence. There are around 6000 dog attacks in the UK every year, some needing hospital treatment and some even fatal. In comparison, about 10 alleged fox attacks are reported every year, and nobody has ever been killed by a fox to my knowledge.

CHAPTER FOUR

Foxyloxy gets a fan club

In the meantime, our Foxyloxy became braver and braver. She gradually came closer and was now eating by the open front door every night while we watched and photographed her. She still would not come anywhere near us when there was a cat nearby. Sometimes, as soon as we called her, the neighbour's two big friendly tomcats showed up too, thinking they might get a nibble of the food. Foxyloxy still seemed scared of these cats, even though she was bigger than they were; it was funny to watch her. Since we wanted to see the fox, there were many evenings when Marcus or Emma picked up the worst offenders, Smudge and Toby, to take them home, before Foxyloxy would come down the path and eat by our front door.

She seemed so friendly now and not a bit scared of us; it was a great opportunity to take many lovely photos of her, which we did every night, squabbling about whose turn it was to hold the camera and whose turn it was to feed her.

I started to show my many photos of her in an album on

Facebook and my friends could not believe that I had a fox in the garden, how near to us she came and how beautiful and friendly she was. Every night I added a few pictures to the album with suitable captions, trying to make them humorous. Many of my friends started to follow the story of Foxyloxy and enjoyed seeing her photos. Some of them wondered if we were ever frightened of her, or if she had ever bitten us. No, we were not scared of her at all; she had never showed any signs of aggression. She was becoming famous among my Facebook friends. Some of my friends were quite jealous, some were horrified and some had never even seen a fox. Well, it takes all sorts, doesn't it? We were enjoying her company.

One night, when she was eating very close to us and remembering Honey at the British Wildlife Centre, I remarked 'I'm sure she would take some food from my hand'. Emma jumped up, ran to the fridge and came back with a chicken drumstick. I thought it would probably be better if I offered it to Foxyloxy myself in case she bit Emma - not that I thought she would, but I didn't really know for sure.

I held the chicken out to Foxyloxy. She was very wary about taking it from me, but of course, she could smell it. I said to her: 'Come on then beautiful, come and get the chicken, come on then girl, it's for you' and other such nonsense. She stretched her neck and sniffed it a couple of times then, finally, snatched it out of my hand!

It was so exciting. The children immediately wanted to do the same and give her something too; they raided the fridge for food and Foxyloxy took a sausage and some more chicken fed by the children. They were not a bit scared of her. Well, that was it; there was no going back now.

We could not believe we had gained her trust enough for her to take food from our hands. It might not have been a great idea to hand-feed her, but it was so much fun and I did not know any better at the time. It set a pattern and during the following nights Emma and Marcus took turns giving her a little bit of food by hand before putting her dish down, usually a piece of chicken or a bit of sausage. She took it so gently and carefully now, no more snatching at all. It was a lovely thing to do, as we could watch her so closely. We only ever gave her a couple of bits of food by hand as we didn't want her to get used to it.

I continued photographing her with the children and adding the photos to my Facebook album. My friends were amazed. At first there were silly comments from them such as 'she'll be sitting on your sofa next' or 'go on, let her in' but before long, they asked if they could come and see her and if they could bring their children to see her.

My Foxyloxy was fast becoming an attraction. Some of the children had never seen a real fox and they were thrilled to see one in real life - this wild animal which they only knew from fairy stories or the TV. Other children saw Emma and Marcus feed her and wanted to do the same; they wanted to feed her too. One boy and his little sister came with their mum and brought her a hardboiled egg. I gave them a fork to put it on, just in case Foxyloxy's teeth came a bit near. She took the egg off the fork and we photographed the occasion of her eating from a fork. Such lovely table manners!

How we laughed at the silly faces she made as she tried to chew her hard-boiled egg; it seemed a bit slippery and kept falling out of her mouth, it was so funny. She did not even mind five of us laughing at her. Some of the children who came took photographs to school to show their teachers and friends that they had fed a real fox! What an education. In fact, I would like to think that I educated not only the children but quite a few adults as well as myself, by showing that foxes were not the vicious, dangerous predators they might have thought.

One night, I saw my neighbour in the garden just as I was feeding Foxyloxy. This woman started screaming when she spotted the fox! Foxyloxy and I were both a bit surprised.

'What are you afraid of?' I asked.

'I think she will come and bite me', the woman said.

'What? Come and bite you, when I am standing here with a chicken leg for her. Now why would she do that?'

She watched me give Foxyloxy her chicken from the safety of her hall, and then she declared that she would now be afraid to go out in the garden in the dark. I never managed to change her mind. In fact, I know this couple do not like animals at all, which does not help; my cats get much the same reaction if they wander up her path. My neighbour must have spent a lot of time indoors during the next year as Foxyloxy started coming during the day - oh dear!

We just had great fun during that summer holiday, with a succession of friends coming at dusk for 'The Foxyloxy Show'. I even had to arrange a rota because, obviously, I did not want to frighten her off by having too many people at the same time; besides, I only have a very small hall. I never gave a guarantee that she would be there - after all, she was a wild animal - but she always appeared at dusk after I called her. Everyone wanted to see her and feed her. She remained gentle and a little wary and no one was ever hurt. She just was not a vicious animal.

She was adorable and strikingly beautiful and her portfolio of photographs was growing on a daily basis. So was her fan base. People followed her story and photographs and I talked about her all the time; it was like having a new baby in the family. She was obsessing me, so much so I even started having nightmares about hunters coming into the street to shoot her. I expect that was because of the ongoing debate in the media about the foxhunting ban. Very upsetting to think somebody would hurt such a gentle animal. I felt very protective of my beautiful wildlife baby who had become my friend.

I also met many more people who feed foxes. Time and again, as I stood waiting in the queue with my dog food at the supermarket checkout or the pet shop, I got into conversation. When asked what kind of dog I owned, I usually confessed: 'I don't have a dog, it's for my fox'. Quite often, the response was 'I feed the foxes too', after which we compared notes and parted as friends. Not once did I hear of an attack on any person, or of another pet being hurt. I did hear of foxes playing with the family dog, though.

Foxyloxy falls in love

The summer passed into autumn, and by October Foxyloxy had become a fully-grown vixen with the most stunning thick red coat and white-tipped brush. Her sweet face and intelligent golden eyes would melt my heart every time I saw her, and her daily visits at dusk remained a wonderful experience. Naturally, as the days grew shorter and shorter, she came earlier and earlier, and when the clocks went back at the end of October, she was here as early as 5 pm. The weather also became colder and wetter, and standing at the open front door was not quite so pleasant. Besides, the thermostat for the central heating is in the hall and the open door caused the heating to work overtime. In addition, Foxyloxy's food was getting wet and I was getting cold. We always had a little conversation, as you do, so feeding her and taking pictures was never a five-minute job. Moreover, I thought it would be a little more discreet as not every neighbour in my road was as pleased as I was to see her, or agreed with my feeding activities.

A permanent awning covers the back of my house; it is always dry under there, and I wondered if it would be better to try to feed her in the back garden under the awning. It was worth a try, so at the right time I sat on the chair outside and called her twice: 'Foxyloxy, dinner time'. Ha! She was such a clever girl; within minutes, she appeared in the back garden. She had used the hole under the garden gate which I had made for my cats years ago. When they were small, one had sprained a paw jumping down from the wooden gate, and because of that injury, I had created a kind of underpass, making it unnecessary for them to jump over it. Foxyloxy now used it too; she was not that much bigger than my cats. In fact, in her thick winter coat she seemed more shiny fur and bushy tail than fox - she was in beautiful condition. It must have been her healthy diet. I never fed her junk food and never ever anything containing chocolate. As with dogs, chocolate is very bad for foxes.

At the end of November and during the December of 2011, fox noises in the night increased again. Screaming and barking woke me regularly in the night and one night when I looked out, as I was wont to do when I heard them, I noticed that she was with a much bigger dog fox. Every night after that I noticed him, following her closely. It seemed that she had an admirer, a boyfriend! In addition, quite often, there was another vixen running around with them. Perhaps that was another member of the local foxy family. I certainly had never seen the other two foxes before. Foxyloxy was easy to recognise, as the white tip to her tail was tiny - no more than two or three inches. The dog fox's tail had at least eight inches of white, while the other vixen's tail was all grey.

I watched the three of them regularly around 2-3 am when I heard them in the road and, whenever I called her name, Foxyloxy stopped dead in her tracks and looked at the house and me. She definitely knew me and seemed torn between coming over or continuing on her way. However, it seemed she was love-struck and snubbed me, preferring to flirt with the dog fox by flouncing her wares and waving her tail seductively. She mostly ignored him as well though. I was astonished, what was she thinking of? She was only 9-10 months old or so.

Later I would learn that foxes become sexually mature at 10 months and only come into season once a year. The vixen will then be fertile for only three days and in anticipation of this event, the dog fox will start to shadow her all the time, ensuring that he will be the one to mate with her when the time is right. He will fight off all other males that come into his territory who try to make a pass at her, as he claims her for his own. Mating generally takes place in late December or early in the New Year.

Aha, that was what all the noises in the night had been. Their screaming and barking is their way of communicating. It is true that they do this all the year round but during the winter months, they become more vocal. Scent marking with urine or faeces is also part of their communication, letting other foxes know about their territory and in the case of vixens, how receptive they are to mating. Most of their sexual activity takes place in winter.

Only the dominant pair of foxes in a family will breed, but there are often other family members around as well; they will not breed but will be there to help look after the cubs by providing food. Sometimes another female in the family group will start to lactate when the cubs are born, and will help to feed the cubs. Goodness, I was learning so much, it was a revelation.

At Christmas, I went to stay with Emma, Marcus, and the rest of my family. I am very lucky to have a lovely neighbour and friend in Jenny, who looks after my animal family whenever I am away: two cats, a tank with tropical fish, garden birds and of course Foxyloxy. I leave plenty of food and she comes over and feeds them all.

However, not all my neighbours are so tolerant of my foxy friend and garden birds; there are some people in the road, who 'hate' all animals, even cats and dogs, calling them disease-ridden, dirty vermin. It is a good thing they do not see me sleeping at night with my two big tabby cats on the bed. Fortunately, I live on my own, so I can please myself. Furthermore, many cat and dog lovers I speak to do the same. I find it very comforting to have two warm furry bodies next to me, one either side. Yes, I know they can be a nuisance, walking all over me, purring loudly, standing on my hair, touching my face, sitting on my pillow and trying to get under the duvet with me on a cold night. If you have ever watched the video clip 'Simon's Cat' on YouTube, you will know exactly what I mean.

On a rainy night, they might come up soaking wet, and with muddy paws; some mornings I am grateful that there was not a medical emergency in the night causing paramedics to rescue me from my bed, as it resembles a dog basket. The shame of it; and for goodness sake, whose idea was it to have white bed linen? I must have been mad. There is a nice, soft, dark-coloured fleece along the end of the bed, which they totally ignore of course, preferring to hem me in towards the top of the bed on the white linen. Did I mention that they are 'classic' tabbies – they are mostly black? Say no more!

When my cats were young, they were in the habit of bringing me 'live' presents in the night – many was the time I rescued a mouse in the middle of the night as they let them go and played with them under the bed, loudly bumping their heads on the wooden slats, which woke me immediately. I almost became more adept at catching mice indoors than the cats. In their old age they do not hunt any longer, which is a relief. Furthermore, they have never killed a bird, and they are 12 years old now.

Around Christmas time, a fabulous surprise present came my way: one of my neighbours, an animal lover, gave me a wonderful book on foxes. It was an illustrated hardback book entitled 'Urban Foxes', written by Professor Stephen Harris and Phil Baker. Both based at Bristol University, they have studied foxes and carried out extensive research on their lives and habits.

I realised this new book was by the author of that first little booklet I had been given months ago at that RSPCA day. I read 'Urban Foxes' from cover to cover; it was fascinating to learn in detail about the behaviour, social interaction, feeding and breeding habits of these gorgeous animals. Moreover, I still refer to it on a regular basis. If only more people would read it, it would do so much to dispel the urban myths that people so willingly believe.

Back to Foxyloxy and her boyfriend. I had wondered if they would mate. During my four-day absence over Christmas that year, Jenny, who was feeding Foxyloxy, assured me that they had, as she had observed them mating right outside her house. It seemed they had not been very discreet. Her text message to me made me laugh out loud. It read: 'Let's say there will definitely be baby foxes next year, you should have heard and seen them!' It made my day. What a brazen hussy! Foxyloxy of course - not Jenny.

The gestation period of a fox is approximately 51-53 days so if she had mated successfully she would probably give birth in late February. I would just have to wait and see. Baby foxes! Such an exciting thought.

After Christmas, I brought Emma and Marcus back home with me for the rest of the school holiday. They were very pleased to see Foxyloxy again, marvelling at how she had grown and wondering if she was pregnant and would have babies. They helped feed her again at dusk and a few times, as I went outside to get the empty bowl back before going to bed, we saw her again by the front door looking for scraps - she did not want to take 'no more' for an answer and seemed very hungry. Unsurprisingly, we gave her some extra bits. The children and I are too soft for our own good and we loved Foxyloxy. She even put a foot over the doorstep every now and then, in order to find the kitchen herself, I think. The photos became increasingly close-up as she became bolder and friendlier and the three of us enjoyed thinking up more amusing captions to accompany the pictures.

She even appeared in broad daylight on the garden table early one afternoon when Emma and a friend were baking cakes; the kitchen door was open and I assumed she had smelled the cakes a mile off. It was Marcus and his friend who spotted her there. 'The fox is here, Foxyloxy is here!' 'She's on the table in the garden!' they shouted excitedly, all thoughts of their game of Yahtzee forgotten in an instant.

They ran outside, but she scarpered and disappeared. How exciting and unusual - we had seen her in the middle of the day. At dusk, she came back for her dinner as always.

One night, Emma and Marcus thought it would be a great idea to put her bowl in the hall. Foxyloxy was very near to us. 'Let's see if she'll come in' they said. Naturally, she did, but I put a stop to that very quickly and told them that inviting Foxyloxy in was not a good idea. 'She is a wild animal and if you let her in she might want to go into other people's houses too and she might not be welcome there'. 'They might hurt her and you would not want that, would you?' They understood my reasoning and, reluctantly, they put the bowl back outside again, but not before she had made a terrible mess with her food on the carpet, messy girl. It was funny to see a fox in my hall though and we managed to take some amazing photographs.

Where's the chicken?

Emma and Marcus went back home again after their holidays and Foxyloxy and I carried on our normal routine during January. It was such a happy time; I loved my new friend. She appeared at the usual times and early one evening, as I came back from putting some papers in the recycling bin, I found her in the hall again. I had left the front door open, silly me - I had not expected her to appear at that time, she must have been hungry. She ran out quickly when I appeared and after that happened, I always made a point of shutting not only the front door but also the door to the living room, as I had visions of finding Foxyloxy lying on the sofa or in front of the fire one day. Not that I would have minded; however, she was a wild animal, and should go about her business and do the things that wild foxes do. It would not be right to encourage her to come in.

I did have a senior moment every now and then, and early one afternoon I forgot to shut the doors again; I remember it vividly. I was carrying my six bags of shopping, in stages, from the car to the kitchen. As I went back out for some more bags, I found Foxyloxy practically sitting in the boot of the car. She was standing on one hind leg with her front legs, head, and shoulders in the car and the other leg on the edge of the boot; she was sniffing at the rest of the shopping. Fortunately, I had already carried the bag containing a hot cooked chicken to the kitchen, or I might well have lost it. I suppose she could still smell it though and wondered where it had gone.

'Hey, what are you doing in my car?' I said, and she ran off. 'You cheeky girl' I called after her. Such a shame I did not get a photo, I thought, but I was so surprised to see her there and so early in the day too.

I took the rest of the shopping from the car into the house, dumped it in the kitchen and then went back to close the car boot and lock the car. I shut the front door and the living room door behind me as I walked back into the room. Then, to my utter disbelief, I found a panicky Foxyloxy in the dining room area running around the table in circles looking for the way out. I realised that she must have come back when I was in the kitchen and had followed me into the house without me noticing. By shutting all the doors, I had trapped her in the room with me.

I froze, not because I was frightened, but because *she* obviously was. I had visions of her hurling herself through the glass doors or window and injuring herself, remembering the French film 'The Fox and The Child' in which the little girl takes the fox home 'to see her bedroom': when the fox finds that it is shut in her bedroom, it jumps through a closed window, thereby getting terribly hurt.

Foxyloxy ran around my room in a panic at finding

herself trapped, frantically jumping on to the sofas, back and forth, onto the coffee table and the dining room table, then back to the patio doors, desperately looking for a way out. I really thought she would injure herself, but I kept very calm, and managed to sidle slowly past her back towards the kitchen door, talking to her all the time. I went outside, leaving the doors open and called her. She found her way out immediately via the kitchen and sat down on the lawn, looking just a bit sheepish but nevertheless relieved to be out again. Phew! We were both a bit shocked, I think.

Foxes have an extremely well developed sense of smell and I had just not given her a single thought. I had not even seen her anywhere in the road when I came home from the supermarket and she had appeared as if by magic; she had an uncanny knack of doing this and she could not have been very far away when she had smelled that chicken and decided to investigate. She must have been really hungry, or maybe she had a bit of a craving?

Talking about food, I had never bought so much chicken; she certainly was not a cheap 'pet' to feed. We shared two cooked chickens every week and, in addition to special offers, I bought cheap sausages, liver and other reduced meat items in the supermarkets, stubbornly refusing to give her junk food such as pizza, doughnuts or sausage rolls. She especially loved chicken, sausages and the occasional egg, along with her daily ration of peanuts and dog biscuits. She was a very spoiled foxy but worth every penny for the pleasure her company, her photographs and her friendship gave to others and myself.

That night Foxyloxy spotted a big fat slug on the patio. I thought she would eat it; she sniffed it, looked at it again, then looked at me with a disgusted expression that said 'I hope you're not expecting me to eat that. Where's my chicken? I know you bought one today.'

By the time I had fetched the camera from the room I was just in time to get a picture of the slug and Foxyloxy's feet. What a shame, I should have had that camera hanging around my neck at all times.

I have since heard that even hedgehogs won't eat slugs if there is other food available. Sometimes, slugs carry lungworm and other parasites which they can pass on. The animals must know instinctively that a slug is not always a healthy option.

CHAPTER SEVEN

Unexplained injury

She continued to surprise and worry me intermittently. One night, she did not come when I called her and during the next three days, I did not see her at all. No matter what time I looked for her, until I went to bed at midnight, she did not appear and her food was left untouched. It did disappear in the night, but I was almost certain that she had not eaten it. Oh dear, what had happened to her? My vivid imagination worked overtime as I imagined her run over on the road or trapped somewhere. Where had she gone?

I walked the woodland lane two, three times a day, calling for her without result, hoping no one would see me or hear me calling her. I cannot imagine now why I was embarrassed at calling her name. I left a couple of biscuits near where there were foxy smells, and where there were signs of fox activity, such as a single shoe, plastic bottles, sandwich trays and a tennis ball. Where could she be?

At night, she did not come for her dinner; none of my neighbours had seen her either. I worried continuously about her, as it was so unusual for her not to come when called after seven months of daily visits.

On the fourth day, she suddenly appeared again at the usual time, about 5:30 pm. She was slowly limping up the path to my front door. I spoke to her gently as I fed her some meat. 'Oh my goodness, what has happened to you girl, where have you been?' I said. Her left hind leg seemed to hurt her and she did not put her foot down on the ground at all. The leg did not seem broken, and as I saw no injury or deformity, I could not understand what was wrong, however something obviously was. I felt very sorry for her. She ate the rest of her food and limped away towards the woodland path. It was a pathetic sight. Obviously, she could not tell me, poor girl: no voice, no choice! I was feeling sick with worry, and by the way, how had I become so horribly attached to her? Had my cat been limping, I would have picked her up and rushed her to the vet straightaway, but what to do with a wild fox?

I needed some advice so I phoned the Fox Project, one of the fox welfare societies mentioned in Stephen Harris' little book. They were a great help. I told them what the problem was and they said that as her leg did not seem to be broken, I should just observe her condition for the moment; she might just have a sprain. Well, that had not even occurred to me. If her condition deteriorated, however, I needed to let them know. In that case, they might be able to cage-trap her as she was such a regular visitor, then bring her back after treatment.

For the time being, I should try giving her Arnica tablets. Arnica is a homeopathic remedy that I happened to be well acquainted with. As a midwife, I have often recommended it for bruising and swelling after childbirth. It was certainly worth a try. Then I had a thought and asked, 'How am I supposed to give a fox a tablet?' I was thinking of the trouble I have with my cats when they have to have a worming pill. They always manage to spit it out when I hide it in their food. On more than one occasion, I have been in danger of serious injury to my fingers after trying to push it down their throat. In fact, one of my friends ended up having three of her fingers stitched after doing just that with her big tomcat.

'Just put it in a honey sandwich' was the reply, 'Foxes have a sweet tooth, they love honey and what is more, as it is a natural antibiotic, honey will also help to heal any wounds or bites'. It made sense, so the next day I bought some Arnica tablets in the Health Food shop in town.

That evening, I made Foxyloxy a Manuka honey sandwich: nice wholemeal bread and butter with two Arnica tablets hidden in it. I know what you are thinking: Manuka honey, the pricey stuff? Well, yes, it was all I had in the house and if it was good enough for me then it would be good enough for Foxyloxy. I cut the sandwich up and fed it to her by hand, before I put the rest of her food down. I did not know at the time that foxes had a sweet tooth - she fell for my 'spiked' honey sandwiches every night. Some evenings she still managed to spit the tiny tablet out, but I would not let her get away with that and always gave her another one, refusing to put her other food down for her until she had taken her medicine. She never did lose condition or her appetite and magically, the treatment seemed to work; after two weeks, she put her foot down every now and then and ten days later on, she walked normally again. It might have been that time had healed her, but I like to think my Arnica and honey sandwiches had helped her. Thank goodness! I was delighted and breathed a sigh of relief. My little friend was as good as new.

Nevertheless, that was not the end of her troubles or my worries about her health, because a couple of weeks after this episode I noticed a wet patch in her fur on her thigh and on the same leg. Initially, I did not think too much about it. However, within three days or so, all the fur in that area fell out, exposing a big, red, open wound. Had she been in a fight or caught her leg on something sharp? Horrified, I made another phone call: 'Hello Fox Project, my fox has a big hole in her back leg, about halfway up, and about 4x3 cm in size', what do I do now?'

Having been given similar advice as before, I resumed the honey and arnica sandwich treatment and observed her carefully. In addition, the Fox Project told me that it was lucky that it was winter or flies might have got into to the wound and laid their eggs in it. Fly strike! Next thing you know there could be maggots in that wound; what a hideous thought. I started making the sandwiches again.

As well as her honey and Arnica sandwiches, I started giving her a little more chicken with her dinner as I thought the extra protein would help her wound to heal; it would also give her a chance to rest as she would not have to spend so much time hunting for additional food. I watched her very carefully and always tried to put her bowl down in such a way that she would have to stand with her left side facing me, enabling me to have good look at her leg.

Foxyloxy herself did not seem unduly worried about this latest injury; furthermore, I heard and saw her jump the fence across the road with no problems at all. She ate her medicated honey sandwiches followed by all her food. In fact, because she seemed more hungry than normal, I wondered if she could be pregnant. In time, the wound closed and healed, although she had scar there for evermore.

Two or three of my neighbours started bringing me their leftovers every now and then, and I was grateful for the discarded sausages and chicken carcasses that came my way; even the odd cottage pie or leftover spaghetti Bolognese were a help, Foxyloxy ate it all. The only thing she ever refused was a banana. It lay on the lawn until it went mouldy. I know now banana is one of the things a dog will not eat either, unless the animal lacks potassium. Naturally, there will always be exceptions to the rule.

Jenny had a special container for leftovers - the lid was marked 'The Foxy Boxy' - but others were not so kindly disposed toward her and I worried about 'my' fox all the time in case somebody would harm her.

My neighbour in the house adjoining mine does not like foxes, or so he says. He rang the doorbell one night. I could see him through the glass and opened the door with trepidation. What would the complaint be this time? Noise? Fouling? I opened the door and there he was with Foxyloxy sitting next to him on the doorstep. Well I never! He had walked her to my house because 'she has been waiting for 10 minutes on the path and you are late with her dinner.' I had not even seen her; she had not been sitting on the lawn. I think my little foxy visitor had charmed him after all. He watched me feed her and even though he did not approve I knew he would never hurt her. He is a big softie at heart really.

Fox or Dog?

The danger in feeding foxes lies in the possibility of them approaching other people who do not like foxes. Foxyloxy only trusted me, and never approached anybody else in the road. She was a one-woman fox. In fact, Jenny, who fed her at my house whenever I was away, never even saw her, yet the minute I arrived back, so did Foxyloxy. She followed me around, found me when I was at a neighbour's house and even sought me out if she heard me talking outside or when I was working in the garden, usually an obvious reminder of the fact that it was coming up to her dinner time.

Once she arrived at my door at the same time as a man delivering the local newspaper. He could not believe his eyes – ignoring him, a fox had walked straight past him and sat on my doorstep. He rang the bell.

'Is that yours?' he asked.

'Oh yes, that is my friendly fox, she has come for her dinner'.

'Is she tame?'

'No, she is a wild urban fox.'

He shook his head in disbelief and told me he had never seen one close up. He watched her eat before continuing his round. Fortunately, he liked foxes and he said he would look out for her and bring her a biscuit next time as I had told him that she liked Hobnobs. 'No chocolate please, that's bad for her', I said. As he was leaving he turned round at the top of the path and asked if he could bring his son to see her – ha, it looked like we had another fan. He did bring his boy the following week. However, despite having seen her previously, and watched how gentle she had been with me, he cannot have been totally convinced; they watched her from the safety of his car.

One evening, she crossed the road with me to say 'hello' to a friend and her little boy; they knew of my fox but had never seen her and they had expressed an interest in meeting her. When Foxyloxy came for dinner a couple of nights later, I just held her bowl up and said 'Come on then, come with me and say hello to my friends, they have not seen you and would like to meet you, come on girl. Heel' I said jokingly as I walked away carrying her bowl and crossed the road. She followed behind me and sat beside me on their doorstep when I rang the bell. Although she looked a little puzzled by the change in routine, she took some chicken from me and stayed. My friends were amazed and delighted. I did not stay very long. I just walked back to my house with her in tow and put her dish down by the door. It was comical the way she had followed me, just like a dog. She ate the rest of the food.

'You are a good girl! That was nice of you, what a lovely girl you are', I praised her. I am sure she knew what I was saying – well, I would like to think so anyway.

Occasionally, other neighbours saw her in the woodland lane, where she would apparently just stand and stare at passers-by from a distance. 'I have just seen your fox' was an often-heard phrase. Your fox! For all I knew they had seen a different one.

I was getting a reputation, and was affectionately known by some as 'that crazy fox lady'. However, one man called me 'you bloody stupid woman'. He considered it was my fault that there were foxes in the road and that they were noisy. The fact they had been there as long as I had lived here and that we were living on the edge of an urban town with fields and woodland all around us mattered not one bit. He even phoned the council, who told him the same more or less and said no, they were not going to do anything about it, because if you removed a fox from its territory, at least three others would move in to fight over it. He did not believe this; this man had only lived in our road for a few months, so as far as he was concerned, the foxes were there because of me.

It is not against the law to feed foxes - although not recommended. I have already mentioned the possibility of them going up to other people. They might be hurt where they would not be welcome. In addition, they may start to rely on the food provided, and if it stops, perhaps because the person feeding them goes on holiday or into hospital, they might wander into another fox's territory. This could lead to terrible fights and even the death of the animal. Furthermore, they might go up to other people's houses. Mind you, leaving Foxyloxy without food during the holidays is not something I would even contemplate. Having said all that, feeding foxes is a wonderful way to observe and photograph them.

For me all that advice came much too late. I could not stop now and I did not want to either; I was too involved. Watching Foxyloxy, caring for her and photographing her had given me a wonderful new hobby and a perfect opportunity to study her. My grandchildren also grew to love Foxyloxy; she was entertaining and educational and enriched our lives.

All through the winter I looked after Foxyloxy, watching her closely, making sure she was all right and giving her food at dusk. As the days were getting longer, she came later and later of course.

In February, I noticed that her front legs were always muddy, and that she came from a different direction at night. I wondered what she was up to now. It looked as if she was digging somewhere, but if so, why?

I referred to my book and concluded that she might be busy looking for or even digging a den, but I had no idea where of course. I studied her carefully; she looked fabulous and, errrm… was it my imagination or was she a little rounder? My grandchildren and I were convinced she was pregnant and that it would not be long before she gave birth. Most cubs are born during March, although there are exceptions, with some being born late February or early April. Oh well, we would just have to wait and see what happened next.

CHAPTER NINE

Cubs on the way

Late February 2012 now and once more, I did not see Foxyloxy for a few days. I was not quite so worried this time because foxes stay with their cubs when they are first born almost all the time and I thought she might now have given birth. I wondered where her den was.

Cubs are born blind and deaf and are unable to maintain their own body heat; they are completely dependent on their mother. Weighing about 100g, they have chocolate-brown fur and little floppy ears and look more like newly-born puppies than foxes. In fact, I heard of people discovering that the abandoned 'puppy' they had found was a fox cub, including a vet! Clearly, if a vet cannot tell the difference, what hope is there for the rest of us? The photographs of newly-born fox cubs in this book make it clear. I am grateful for those charities which have let me use their pictures to show you what a very young fox cub looks like.

A vixen will rarely leave her cubs in the first couple of weeks; she stays in the den, curls her tail around them to keep them warm and suckles them, only leaving them for short periods to urinate or defecate outside the den. A cub's eyes open around 11-14 days. They are blue in colour at first; the dark fur will then become more russet-coloured starting from the head, the ears will prick up and the face becomes more elongated, giving them the typical foxy appearance. They grow rapidly on the rich milk that the vixen produces, so that by 12 weeks they look like miniature versions of their mother.

During the early days after giving birth, the vixen is entirely dependent on the dog fox or another member of her family for food. They will bring her food during this time and leave it outside or near the den, as she will not tolerate the dog fox near her cubs.

Certainly, my offerings of food disappeared every night, although I did not see Foxyloxy, the dog fox or the other 'spare' vixen that had been with her during December.

I was still not sure that Foxyloxy had given birth. However, after several days of absence, she returned to see me. I studied her carefully to see if she looked thinner, and looked for signs of lactation. When a vixen gives birth and starts to produce milk, she loses all the fur from her belly, revealing a row of swollen teats, but far as I could see, Foxyloxy looked as she always did, so I was still not sure she had cubs. She ate her food very quickly and disappeared straightaway in the direction from where I had seen her coming a few weeks earlier when I had wondered if she was digging a den. She came to me again the next night and did the same – ate quickly and ran away down the road in the same direction. As it was dark, I did not even get a good look at her.

A few days later however, she appeared in the back garden in the afternoon; I found her sitting up on my garden chair. What is more, I could clearly see a row of swollen teats on her bare belly. There was no doubt about it now, she had cubs after all and was producing lots of milk to feed them. I was over the moon. 'Oh what a clever girl, you have had your babies and you are feeding them, what a good mummy', I said, as I gave her the bowl of food. She appeared ravenous, emptied the bowl very quickly and ran away. Maybe her mate had not brought her much food.

I told Emma and Marcus about the cubs and spread the news excitedly among my friends. I felt like a new grandmother announcing the birth of a grandchild, probably more than one. We all wondered how many cubs there were, where she had hidden them and whether or not she would bring them to me here. I could not wait - I had never seen cubs before, apart from Foxyloxy herself of course. She never stayed long during the last couple of weeks of that March, just came for quick visits to eat her dinner.

By April, Foxyloxy had started to look very scruffy. Her tail, which had once been so luxurious, seemed thinner, and so was the rest of her fur, which had always been so thick and shiny. Being a mother had obviously taken it out of her. I also noticed she ate very little herself and had started to take food away with her. What was happening now? Was she taking food to the cubs? She also appeared tired and nervous, always looking to the same side of my garden; maybe she could hear them? She even jumped up on the roof of the shed to look in that direction.

Often I would find her lying down on the lawn, on the garden table or on my sun lounger for a quick rest.

Furthermore, she continued to take food away. I was astonished how much food she could fit into her mouth; it was hilarious to watch her trying to get more and more in her mouth. When she dropped bits, she would go back repeatedly to pick them up and cram them in again. On one occasion, I videoed her doing this, and when I showed the clip to my friends it created many comments and laughs. People could not believe what they were seeing; I reckoned that she could have fitted a whole chicken in her mouth.

I still worried about her coat though; as the days passed, she started to look so scruffy that I thought she was getting mange, a nasty skin condition caused by mites burrowing under the skin. In severe cases, it can cause them to lose all their fur. It is immensely irritating and causes them a great deal of suffering. It is a condition which in four months can result in death. I did not want to think about it, but had to be sure. Moreover, as soon as a hosepipe ban in this area came into force in April, because of the preceding two dry winters, the weather took a turn for the worse. To be exact, the heavens opened and it rained and rained nearly every day for the next nine weeks. Consequently, my little furry friend was often very wet when she arrived, which made her look worse than ever.

I emailed her photo to The Fox Project to ask them what was wrong with her. Back came the answer: 'she is moulting!' Well I never! I had not even thought of that - I guess I did not remember everything written in my book. Apparently, foxes do not moult during their first year, but every year after that they do. In April, they start shedding their long old winter coat and start growing a new one. The cubs also pull their mother's fur out during feeding and playing. The Fox Project assured me that by the end of summer she would have a new shorter coat; her fur would then grow longer and thicker so that by the time winter came it would be just like before. My book said the same when I looked it up - oh thank goodness, it was just a moult.

However, The Fox Project advised me on some homeopathic mange treatment, 'just in case', so I bought some. Mind you, this would only be effective if she was no more than 40% affected, which she certainly was not. I did not really see any bare patches in her coat, but I was not prepared to take any chances. If she was getting mange, she could infect her cubs. This time, the recommended medication was arsenicum and sulphur, combined in one tablet, so I knew I was going to have to make 'spiked' sandwiches again for a while. Even if she did not have mange, it would do no harm to her or the cubs. Foxyloxy loved her daily sandwiches with strawberry jam or honey and always ate them herself before getting her food and taking some away.

The National Fox Welfare Society is another charity which treats affected foxes very successfully for mange; they will even send you the medicine free of charge, providing you are willing to feed the foxes. I have included more information about their work and that of other wildlife charities at the end of this story.

By now, Foxyloxy had just a mane of long red fur around her neck; she resembled a lion. I saw no bare skin, just very scruffy fur, a raggedy tail, and darker areas where the new coat was beginning to grow. I gave her the medicine for four weeks in the end, by which time I was convinced she did not have mange.

During early May, I was always able to have a good look at her as she sat or lay on the table or in my chair under the awning in broad daylight, I continued to photograph and video her. It was nice and dry there of course. Sometimes when she yawned, which she did a lot, I could see how big her mouth really was; I also saw her 42 shiny white teeth and fangs, making it even more endearing that she had never once hurt any of us; it just showed how very gentle she was.

Every day Foxyloxy took a great deal of food away for her cubs, so I guessed she was weaning them. In that case, I estimated they were about 7-8 weeks by now and still I did not know where she had hidden them, though all this was about to change.

Meeting the family

Mid May, because she had been ill, I went to visit my sister in Holland. I was away for five days and, as usual, Jenny looked after Foxyloxy and the rest of the animals at my house. My fridge contained two cooked chickens as well as a variety of other foods, such as sausages and raw chicken wings to keep them going. I knew my mama fox and her cubs would not go hungry. As usual, Jenny did not see her at all during my absence, although the food disappeared from my garden every night.

Yet again, the minute I was back, so was Foxyloxy, waiting on the path in front of my house as soon as she heard me talking to my neighbours. It was remarkable. She just plodded over, walked home with me and waited patiently on the garden table while I prepared her food. I was so pleased to see her, I had really missed her – I would like to think that she was pleased to see me too.

She put her nose on my hand when I put the bowl down and I had to resist the strong urge to stroke her head. I do not think she would have let me in any case; she obviously knew me well but had always remained a little aloof. Just as well, I suppose. Actually, unexpected movements easily spook all wild animals. As long as I sat still or walked slowly towards her she was fine, but if I dropped something or threw the newspaper down, or sneezed even, she flinched and backed off.

I resumed the normal feeding routine with her in my back garden and I noticed how she always disappeared with the food in her mouth the same way down the road. Moreover, she was back within minutes for more food; I reasoned that her den could not be that far away, so I started to feed her near the front door, in order to spy on her.

One evening I saw her turn right before the end of the road, into a passageway between two houses. She went the same way the following night and the night after that. Her den was definitely nearby; it was probably in the garden of one of those two houses, no more than 30 yards down the road. The following day, I decided to investigate. The first house seemed the most likely, because there was fencing all around the garden.

I know the man who lives in the first house. He is not often around, but I saw him coming home that afternoon and walked over to speak him. 'How do you feel about foxes?' I asked hesitantly, as I was not sure what he would say, 'it's just that I think you may have a den in your garden'.

'Oh, I know I have' he said, 'It is under my shed and there are four cubs too'.

What a surprise!

'Four cubs, have you seen them then?'

'Yes, I see them nearly every day' he said. 'They are

under my shed and come out every now and then to play outside the den. I have been taking photographs, but they are very shy and run away when they see me. I have seen the mother coming home with food quite often – somebody must be feeding her.'

Ha! That was funny. I told him how she had been coming to my house for over a year now and that I had been feeding her.

I could feel my heart beating fast when I asked him if I could come and see the cubs and he invited me to come in and see them straightaway. First I ran home to get my camera. He had already mentioned that they were very shy, so I understood when he said that we could not actually go and see them in the garden; we would have to look at them from his spare room. My heart was pounding with anticipation and excitement as we went up the stairs; would they be outside the den for me to see?

I looked out of the open window and there were the cubs - all four of them, and Foxyloxy was with them. How wonderful! She had dug her den under his rickety old shed and had given birth there all by herself.

At the sight of those four impeccable little mini-foxes, I was overwhelmed with emotion. They were so beautiful, so perfect, and these were Foxyloxy's babies. It was mind-blowing to see them after all this time, and it was worth every penny I had ever spent on buying chicken and all the other food for her. These innocent little bundles of downy fur must have been about 10 weeks old; they were bigger than I thought they would be, already looking like proper little foxes, fat and healthy, and all slightly different.

They were rolling around, play fighting, and chasing

each other, jumping on their mother, nibbling her ears and her tail, pouncing on her, pulling her fur, and biting each other. It was comical to watch. One of the cubs, the largest one, had the most gorgeous black front legs and I named him 'Sox'. Two of the other well-grown cubs had lighter patches on their flanks and were always together. The fourth cub was a smaller, timid one. That little one must have been the runt of the litter. Clearly, from the way they behaved, a hierarchy had already been well and truly established.

Whenever I watched the cubs, which I did very often in the following weeks, this little one was always last in line when Foxyloxy came back with food; the bigger ones grabbed it first and ran off with it to hide it or eat it away from the little cub.

Sox was the most assertive and dominant of them all, always waiting for his mother on the path outside the den and snatching food from her mouth as soon as she came back. I decided he must be a boy. Foxyloxy would softly bark to let the other cubs know she was back. The little one quite often did not seem to get any of the chicken that Foxyloxy brought back. It would nibble its mother's face begging for food while the others were eating, and would then stick closely to her. Sometimes, Foxyloxy let it have a quick suckle instead. At 'playtime', it was always last out of the den as well, peering anxiously out from the entrance while the three boisterous siblings were already playing. I read in my book that a vixen will get rid of the dominant cub and the runt of the litter first, keeping one or two of the others. Often a little one would not make it to adulthood. How sad, it was such a perfect baby. Nature can be very cruel; it is indeed survival of the fittest.

The garden they were all in was quite unkempt, with empty pots, broken chairs and other rubbish lying around, and there were lots of brambles and overgrown bushes. It included a little pond and I saw them drinking from it; that garden was a fox's paradise and a perfect playground for those little ones. In order to get to her den Foxyloxy leapt six feet on to the fence from the garden next to it and then walked down a plank supporting that fence on the other side.

Some of my gossipy neighbours were convinced that there was another reason for my evening visits to this house, armed with my camera as I was. Well, if that is what amused them, so be it. Understandably, I had not told everyone about the cubs, only the neighbours whom I trusted.

Around this time Channel 4 broadcast a marvellous TV programme 'Foxes Live: Wild in the City'. There were discussions, films, interviews and even 'live' webcams outside dens in several locations in people's gardens; it was compulsive viewing for many people and, of course, for me. It did a great job of raising the profile of urban foxes in this country. As fans we all wondered what on earth we were going to watch after the series ended and we speculated about the fate of the little cubs we had seen. Yes, we would sorely miss our foxy fix on TV.

However, during the four-part series, a woman viewer on the on-line forum suggested setting up a special group on Facebook, 'Fox Watch', where those who loved foxes would be able to continue to share photos, news and stories about foxes after the end of the series. I joined straightaway; after all, I had many photos to share and stories to tell. It proved a great idea; many more people from all over Britain joined the group.

After the hugely successful and popular 'Foxes Live' series ended, the name of the group changed to Nature Watch - not everybody had foxes around, although many members of the group wished they had. At the time of writing this story, there are some 2200 members from all over Britain, plus quite a few from abroad as well. New people are joining every day, so we see a large variety of wildlife and nature, as all our interests are different. We marvel at the amazing nature photos and stories from the professional photographers in the group. Others are enthusiastic amateurs like me who photograph not only all their garden visitors but flowers, parks, walks, nature trails, landscapes and animals at wildlife reserves in their areas.

Expert or amateur, we all share this interest in nature and can ask for identification or advice on a wide variety of subjects, as quite a few members are experts. Thus, we learn from each other and have a lot of fun as well. I have learnt so much since I became a member and the old adage 'you learn something new every day' is certainly true within this friendly group. For example, I can identify many more birds now than I could a year ago and even if I do not always remember them the week after, in time the information tends to stick. My contribution to the group consists usually of the identification of plants and flowers for others, and of course I post photos of the birds, foxes, hedgehogs and even frogs visiting my garden.

I have always liked taking photos, but photography has played a much bigger part in my life since becoming a member of the group and since having such a willing and stunning model. After all, as the saying goes, 'you've got to have a hobby'. Especially as I have now retired.

Photos of foxes remain popular and unsurprisingly, we are all against animal cruelty or a repeal of the foxhunting ban. We cannot understand why anyone would want to hurt such an enchanting animal.

I was by no means the only person with urban foxes in the garden, but in those early days of the group I had one of the most friendly and photogenic ones. Foxyloxy was a right poser and continued to delight and surprise many people with her shenanigans and adventures around my house and garden. People loved the photos and video clips I showed them of her; Foxyloxy and her cubs used to get many flattering comments. They certainly were a fine example of one of Britain's most attractive and indigenous wild animal species, the Red Fox.

Hello foxy, aren't you beautiful. My first photo of Foxyloxy

Coming closer....

The most beautiful creature

The house from the road

The road to the left of the house

The fence and hedge opposite the house

Worth stepping inside for

Messy eater

An irresistible offer from Emma - a piece of chicken

The Foxyloxy Show - Marcus feeds her with a fork

That was yummy!

Dog biscuits with lavender

Don't try and pull the wool over my eyes, I know you bought a chicken today

Foxyloxy after having her cubs - notice the full teats

Big boobs, shame about the coat

I'm not eating that, it's spiked

Soaking wet and moulting - not a good look

Foxy Loxy's lion impression

A scruffy mum and two of her beautiful babies

Three of the four cubs outside the den

Sox at 12 weeks, waiting for his mum

The runt of the litter at 12 weeks - she still has blue eyes

Surely you're not drinking that green stuff

A tired mum soaks up some rays after a nine-week downpour

I can hear them, you know

Do you mind if I use your table?

A take-away to help wean the cubs

An egg to help restore her coat

Are you having a laugh?

Who left all those feathers on the lawn then?

An after-dinner snooze in the sun lounger

Open wide - 42 lovely white gnashers on display

Where's my food?

So glad I found you at home

Really nice of you to share your chicken

Look at that muddy nose... she's been burying food to teach the cubs to forage

Ever had the feeling someone is watching you?

I can't believe you didn't lay a place for me

Steal your purse....me?

Watching, listening, waiting

Don't worry, I'll soon have that egg cleared up

Can I have a biscuit too?

Hobnobs, my favourite!

A slice of birthday cake

That'll be 4, 7, 7, 9, 2, 8

A girl can never have too much chicken

A pigeon! There's gotta be a catch

Waiting by the front door after our holiday in Holland

She had a lovely new coat by the end of August

The last time Foxyloxy walked up to my door

Last sighting of Foxyloxy

My glorious girl. Thank you Foxyloxy, it was a privilege to know you

My picture on the BBC website

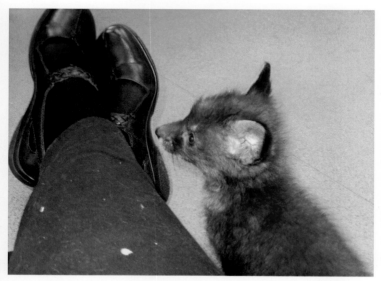

A fox cub at The Fox Project checks out my shoes - for future reference

A newly-born cub, umbilical cord still attached (photo by South Essex Wildlife)

I met eight-week-old Hermione at the Fox Project

Newborn fox cub (photo National Fox Welfare Society)

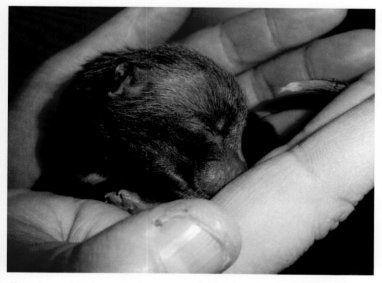

Even a vet mistook this cub for a kitten! It's Julian (photo by The Fox Project)

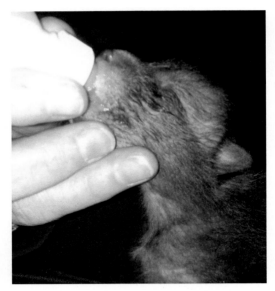

Julian gets his three-hourly bottle feed (The Fox Project)

At two weeks, Julian's eyes are open and red fur is
beginning to show (The Fox Project)

Julian at 12 weeks, in an outdoor pen (The Fox Project)

Foxyloxy and the handbag

Early June now, and Foxyloxy started coming during the day. She would appear during the morning or afternoon or both, and always in the evening. I really looked forward to her visits. When sitting indoors, I sometimes had the feeling someone was watching me. On looking up, I would see Foxyloxy sitting on the garden table looking at me through the glass doors. The look on her face said 'you are not in there having something to eat without me, are you?'

Foxyloxy was a fabulous mother. The way she looked after her cubs was touching, she hardly ate herself and always listened out for them when she was with me; she must have been able to hear them from my garden. When she was here, she sometimes jumped up on the shed roof for a better look and listen. She let them clamber all over her. She groomed them and still let them suckle occasionally, which she now did while standing up.

When she was here, she was mostly just mooching around the garden - sitting or lying in my chair, on the lawn, or asleep on the table, She was just having a break from her children I guess, as they were becoming increasingly boisterous and vocal. Furthermore, it would appear she was a single mother, as I never saw any other foxes near her. It must have been hard work.

If I sat in the garden with the papers, she would suddenly join me, sniffing the paper, my hands, my shoes, my teacup and my chair. Some days she tried to climb up on the chair with me, making me think she was going to sit on my lap; at other times she would just curl up in the other sun lounger and watch me, or go to sleep. What surprised me was that she had no smell - no Eau de Reynard on her. I will not linger on her occasional habit of marking her food dish with urine or a smelly poo – charming! She never 'marked' my garden chair as hers though – I think she knew it was mine really.

One morning, as I sat in the sun on the patio with a friend enjoying coffee and biscuits, Foxyloxy suddenly arrived in the garden. 'Hello, darling', I said. Totally ignoring my friend, she came over to me, sniffed my shoes and even had a little nibble of one. Foxes tend to explore with their mouths but maybe she wanted to take it away as a toy for her cubs. Unluckily for Foxyloxy, my foot was in it, so no taking that one with her. She sat next to my chair looking at me expectantly, licking her mouth, and putting on her best 'begging' expression.

'Perhaps you would like a biscuit too?' I suggested. She willingly accepted a Hobnob, rendering my friend speechless, and ate it, then asked for another one by sniffing and licking my hand, then her mouth again. She may not have been able to talk, but the message was loud and clear.

I gave her another one. How could I resist her? She was impossibly beautiful, and totally adorable. Nonetheless, she was also full of mischief, as we shall see.

The day before the Queen's Diamond Jubilee celebrations started, I brought my washing in from the garden, folded it all up outside and popped in through the patio door to put it upstairs. It was around 5.30 pm on the Friday. I cannot have been much more than five minutes upstairs, but when I came down my black handbag was on the lawn. That confused me: had somebody been in my house? I checked the garden gate: there was nothing wrong, the lock was secure and there was no one in the garden.

I went to retrieve the bag, the shoulder strap of which was now torn in five pieces, and found the contents of the bag strewn on the lawn. While picking up all the bits and pieces, Foxyloxy suddenly appeared in the garden and looked at me. She came over to see what I was doing, and then she sniffed the bag. It was immediately clear to me who had committed the offence, despite the innocent look on her face.

'Did you do that by any chance, you naughty girl? Did you steal my handbag while my back was turned?' I asked her. As I started to gather up all the bits and pieces, I noticed my bag felt very light and, as I looked inside, I was horrified to discover my purse was missing. 'Oh, you are a bad girl, you little red thief!' I said. 'Have you stolen my purse? What have you done with it? Bad fox!'

She wore an expression that plainly said 'who, moi?' but she did not deceive me - I just knew I was looking at the culprit and that she had taken my purse away. All in the five minutes or so I had needed to take the washing upstairs – unbelievable. Clearly it had been another of her 'as if by magic' appearances, as she had not been anywhere in sight when I went upstairs. It was obvious that she had sneaked in through the open patio door. The bag had been by the side of the sofa.

I was flabbergasted; I could not believe what had just happened: she had taken my purse away, but where? Perhaps she had buried it. I started looking around the garden, where I had often noticed her burying bits of food – nothing. I searched the front garden, the plant pots and all the neighbour's gardens, to my left, to my right – nothing. I walked to the house where she had her den. The owner was in.

'Have you seen Foxyloxy coming back with my purse in her mouth?' I asked. 'I think she might have taken it as a toy for her cubs.' After all, he often saw her coming back with food. He looked puzzled and asked me what had happened. No, he had seen not seen her and no, when we searched there was nothing anywhere in his garden or in any of the back gardens near the den or of those backing on to the den for that matter.

Despite the obvious inconvenience, we burst out laughing at the thought of a fox stealing my purse and carrying it away. I told him what it looked like and asked him to keep an eye out for it. If it were under his shed, I would probably stand no chance of finding it unless the rickety thing fell down, but you never know.

As I could not be sure of the whereabouts of my purse now, I had no other choice but to cancel all my credit and debit cards and wave goodbye to my driving licence, bus pass, store cards, stamps, loyalty cards and £35 in cash. The thing might have been down the lane, where anyone could have picked it up. Various card issuers reassured me that no money had been spent since the day before when I had been shopping for the Bank Holiday weekend. I also asked my neighbours to look out for it, but I did feel a bit foolish as I thought they would probably say 'serves you right for befriending her'. Mostly they laughed.

Everyone thought it was a huge joke. My Facebook friends in the Nature Watch group had hysterics when I told them what had happened. 'I've seen her on the bus with your bus pass', 'she was wearing your lipstick', 'she's gone to buy a new Gucci bag with your credit card' and 'she's gone to the supermarket to buy more chicken' were some of the sympathetic comments. I read them with tears in my eyes from laughing, it seemed so funny! The thought of her nipping into the house quick as a flash, dragging the bag outside, chewing it and then walking off with my purse was just too comical. Besides, that purse was heavy. I would never live it down.

I checked the DVLA website and found out it would cost me £25 for a replacement licence. I tried to apply, but their web page was 'temporarily unavailable'. As it turned out that was just as well; as, astonishingly, five days later, the lodger who lived in the house where the den was saw my purse from upstairs in the long grass in the garden next to his. He brought it back. It was complete with fang marks but the contents were intact. Foxyloxy had not been shopping after all. She must have dropped it as she jumped the fence to her den. I told you it was heavy.

Unfortunately, I could not use any of my cards now as I had cancelled them all, but I had my driving licence back, as well as the bus pass, the cash and all the other bits and pieces a woman keeps in her purse. Due to the four-day

Jubilee holiday, new cards and PIN numbers took 10 days to arrive, which was a nuisance, but as I had been shopping before the holiday, I did not need them anyway. In any case, a couple of kind friends offered to lend me money till the new cards arrived and the bank offered me an emergency PIN which would have enabled me to get money out of my account at an ATM. I didn't realise banks could do that. As I have said before, you learn something every day.

All's well that ends well, and I knew now that I could definitely not trust Foxyloxy with an open door in my absence - even if it was just for a minute, and even if she was nowhere in sight. Behind her sweet adorable face, there lurked a mischievous thieving mind, and I was extra vigilant from then on.

Naturally, Foxyloxy turned up and attended the Jubilee celebrations that weekend as well. My neighbours and I had organised a street party. About 24 adults, one guide dog-in-training, plus 14 children and babies were all having a nice time eating, drinking, chatting and playing games, when all of a sudden I had that feeling of being watched again. I looked around and there was Foxyloxy, sitting in a garden opposite us, just watching the celebrations. I do not know how long she had been sitting there; nobody had noticed her, not until I mentioned it anyway, and I had not seen her arrive. I called her and she started to walk towards me. Some of the smaller children got a bit excited and ran towards her to get a better look. She backed off immediately.

At that precise moment, the dog noticed her too and jumped up excitedly, thereby pulling over a chair because his lead was around the arm of the chair. The dog's owner, who was sitting on that chair, fell to the floor entangled in the lead and chaos ensued! Food and drinks went flying as people rushed to help her up and restrain the dog. Everyone bar the children forgot about the fox.

'Don't run at the fox, I know her', I warned the children. 'If you want to see her, just stand still while I go up to her, I will call her'.

I took a few sausages and a sandwich and walked over to Foxyloxy, who had sat down again a bit further away. She munched the food I gave her with everybody watching her from a little way away and then strolled off down the lane. Everyone saw how gentle she was. We all sat down again and then had a good laugh as I retold the story of the stolen purse. Oh yes, she was a source of great entertainment, it has to be said.

She could be impatient as well. I was videoing her from the kitchen one day as she was mooching round in the garden. It was her dinnertime, so her bowl was ready, next to me on the floor. I was crouching on the floor in the doorway with the camera. Suddenly she ducked under my arm, pushed me out of the way and made off with a mouth full of food. I gave up and laughed at her nerve. 'I was going to give it you, you cheeky girl'. I still have that video clip and even now, it makes me smile. She was quick as a flash!

The cubs were quickly growing bigger and ran her ragged, and she started to spend more and more time in my garden away from them; she looked drained. Not only that, but because it was still raining on and off, she often would turn up wet as well, making her look even more dishevelled. I think she came to have a rest from her family, and to dry out under my awning. I would find her curled up on the garden table, on the lawn, in my sun-lounger or on the patio looking in through the doors; her numerous visits led to many beautiful photos of her. She was a model poser. However, despite the fact that I could now see new fur growing on her, she still looked tatty, with her once beautiful tail resembling a shredded piece of string.

I thought an egg might help her coat. She gently took it from my hand and immediately carried it away – to give to her cubs, no doubt. Later on that week, after half a dozen or so eggs had gone that way, I started breaking an egg in a bowl so she could not take it away; from then on, she ate them herself, so I gave her one every other day until her coat improved.

On my birthday, we celebrated with a piece of my cake and an egg. She hung around the garden on and off that afternoon, investigating my newspaper, and jumping on the end of the sun-lounger I was sitting in; again, I thought she was going to sit on my lap – dream on! She was just nosey. She settled down on the garden table, after nervously staring at my cats; and finally, when she was sure they were not going to attack her, she fell asleep.

CHAPTER TWELVE

The family breaks up

Early July, in the middle of the afternoon, Foxyloxy walked down the road with her biggest cub 'Sox' by her side, and went towards the woodland lane. I wondered where she was going and why she was only with one cub. It looked as if she was taking him somewhere else, and indeed, I never saw him again after that day. Perhaps she thought he was old enough to fend for himself, or perhaps she took him to live with his father and the rest of her family. Male cubs often go and live with the dog fox. Who knows? He must have been only four months or so, the same age Foxyloxy had been when her mother vanished.

I have learnt that from late summer onwards the bonds in a family group start to weaken; perhaps Sox's disappearing was the start of this. Yes, he was a big cub, but it seemed a bit early as my book told me that foxes start to disperse in autumn, when they are fully-grown young adults, and it was only June. I often wonder what became of this most beautiful, bold young fox. I do hope he had a safe and happy life, living wild and free.

When the cubs are older, I do know that the vixen will abandon the den and start to lie up in the bushes or under brambles during the day, sometimes away from the cubs. There were plenty of brambles down the lane. The cubs also will spend less and less time with the vixen as they explore their surroundings and learn to hunt for themselves.

Worldwide research so far has failed to establish exactly how and when fox cubs leave their family. Is has been suggested that female cubs have stronger bonds to the mother and often a vixen will keep one or two female cubs with her to help her rear the next litter of cubs the following year. The male cubs will leave and have to find a new territory. Well, actually, their father will usually send them packing, as this ensures that younger males do not breed with his mate.

One of my friends who also has foxes in her garden, mentioned that her vixen, Fifi, had had two cubs around the same time that Foxyloxy had hers. The young female cub, Star, is friendly like Fifi. She has stayed with her, and still visits every day; the young male cub, Indi, mostly hangs around with his dad, Russell, and only comes in the night.

Funny how we give foxes names, just as you would with any other household pets. I know they do this at the Fox Project as well – they say it is easier to refer to cubs and foxes that come in to their hospital by name instead of by number. It is also quite humorous; foxes and cubs often have names relating to the area in which they are found, or a name connected to the person or persons who found them. The work they do at this charity and many others is amazing; I believe during 2012 the Fox Project cared for approximately 650 foxes. They cared for abandoned cubs, bottle-feeding them three-hourly when necessary, and treated victims of accidents, disease and cruelty. They created new family groups and found foster families for others; they successfully treated sick foxes and nursed them back to health prior to releasing them back to the territory where they were came from, and found new release sites for others. In addition, they advised thousands of people on a variety of issues such as healthcare, behaviour and humane deterrence. During a talk I attended at their headquarters this year, the director told us of a man who wanted them to get rid of a fox that frequented his garden because 'it drinks out of my pond and I don't like it'. Such a shame, he does not know what he is missing. He did not even have any fish in it!

I checked on Foxyloxy's remaining three cubs, to find that they were all still at the den. They were getting out of their own garden more these days, and often they were playing in the one next door. The woman who lived there said she had seen the cubs playing with her cats on more than one occasion. That was a surprise; I already knew that Foxyloxy herself seemed scared of the local cats and now her cubs were playing with the cats living there? Amazing! So much for the myth that foxes attack cats. By now, there were 13 cats in the 19 houses in this small cul-de-sac and I never once saw a fox chase one of the cats or heard of a cat hurt by one of the foxes around here.

Foxyloxy herself moved house too and no longer visited the den. Her large cubs had become increasingly vocal as they grew up, so peace now returned to the garden where they had lived. Jenny had seen her marching her remaining three cubs along the road and across into a garden somewhere opposite my house, behind a fence. The man who lives there said he used to see the cubs and the mother playing on his trampoline. I asked him if he had any photographs as I would have loved to have seen that, but he didn't. It looked as if Foxyloxy and her three cubs were living there now and I assumed the rest of her family were still down the lane. I did not see her mate, Sox or the other vixen again either. I hoped they were all safe.

Foxyloxy continued to look after the remaining three cubs with dedication; they were five months old and almost bigger then she was now. She herself had remained a small fox, even though she was about 17 months old now.

As a result of her house move, I did not see the cubs in daylight again, which was a shame, as I obviously could not take any more photos of them. My night-time camera skills are non-existent. When Foxyloxy now visited me at dusk, I saw her burying bits of chicken all over my garden, in the back, in the front, in the borders and in my neighbour's plant pots. She dug a little hole with her front paws, dropped the food in it and then pushed the soil back with her nose; it was comical to see her muddy face. She started bringing her three cubs to my house under cover of darkness every night. I watched her sitting or lying under the lamp post on the grass across the road, keeping an eye on her cubs while they searched for the buried food and argued noisily with each other. Occasionally, they would run back to their mother, nuzzling up to her for reassurance. She would lick and groom them and fuss over them, after which they would run back and continue their search for bits of chicken, peanuts and sandwiches. She called them back if she thought they were in danger, for example when somebody walked down the road or when a car came into the road;

and in a flash, they would be nowhere to be seen. They continued their play fighting and squabbling among themselves. It was so special to watch this little family together. I loved it, and every night around 11pm when I heard them, I would look out of the window and observe them for an hour or so. It was definitely the highlight of my day to see them all.

Breakfast fox

Although she only ever brought the cubs at night, Foxyloxy herself could arrive any time of day. As I was cooking breakfast one morning with the kitchen door open, she turned up at 8am, the earliest I had ever seen her here. She just sat on the back door step and watched me cooking my egg and bacon with an expectant look on her face. 'I suppose you would like an egg for your breakfast too?' I said, as I turned around to grab another egg out of the box on the opposite counter. I was going to give her the egg whole in its shell, but it slipped out of my hand and fell to the floor, breaking on the kitchen mat. Her face was a picture.

'What happened to my egg?' she seemed to say, staring at the mess on the mat.

'Oh dear, you had better clean that up' I told her. She did not need telling twice. She stepped into the kitchen and licked the broken egg off the mat while I took a photo of her standing there. I did not think anyone would have believed me otherwise. When she had finished, she walked out and sat in my garden chair, quite happily watching me eat my breakfast. OK, I gave her a piece of my toast as well and then she went home, wherever that was. I asked myself how many people were having breakfast with a fox for company, not many, I bet! I loved her companionship; she was captivating.

A few days later, I heard a terrible screeching noise in my garden about mid-morning. I shot up from the sofa and ran outside, expecting the worst. Oh god, where were my cats? Phew, they were both in the living room, so it could not be them. With trepidation, I went outside to investigate.

On the lawn in the back garden sat a big white and tabby cat with a feral pigeon in his jaws, and the poor thing was screeching. 'NO!' I shouted and ran towards the cat. Frightened by my shouting, the cat dropped the pigeon and rushed off. There were feathers everywhere, with the shocked pigeon lying on the grass among them. I carefully picked it up and examined it; it was still alive but it was gasping, poor thing. It had two puncture marks on its breast, as well as marks on its back where the cat had grabbed it and, as I stood there contemplating what I should do with it and stroked its head, it closed its eyes, went limp and died.

I was shaking with the shock of it. I had seen that cat previously; he was almost invisible sitting under the low branches of one of my shrubs. It must have been hiding there again. I was furious, especially as my own cats have never touched one of my garden birds. They just sit and 'yakker' at the pigeons. I grabbed the secateurs and trimmed every low branch off that shrub; I could now see right underneath and past it, so no more hiding there for that cat. I know it is their nature to chase birds, but cats are fed at home and do not need to kill to eat, unlike foxes. That gave me an idea. Instead of burying the pigeon or throwing it away, I would give it to Foxyloxy when she came that evening. That way the pigeon's death would not have been in vain, so I wrapped it in some newspaper and kept it out of sight in the kitchen.

During the afternoon, one of my friends visited with her six-year-old son. He noticed all the feathers on the lawn. 'Why are there feathers all over your garden?' he asked.

'What do you think has happened there?' I replied.

'Has your cat caught a bird?'

'No, not my cat, but the neighbour's cat, he killed a pigeon'.

He picked some of the feathers up, examined them, and then asked 'where is it now?' I told him I was keeping it to give to Foxyloxy for her dinner. He knew Foxyloxy, as he was one of the children who had fed her the previous summer and had seen her many times after that. Being a very inquisitive little boy, he wanted to see the dead pigeon. I asked his mum if it would be all right to show it to him and with her permission, I showed him the bird. He was fascinated. We examined it together and he stretched the wings out to admire the feathers and the lovely colours. He saw the puncture marks and asked if that was why the bird had died. 'Yes, that and the shock of it all', I replied. Satisfied that he knew the full story and with his feathers safely tucked in his Mum's handbag, he washed his hands and had a drink, waiting for Foxyloxy, as it was near her dinnertime by now. I gave my friend the camera and asked her if she would take a picture of me giving Foxy her 'special present', just for the records.

Before long, Foxyloxy turned up; she came towards me by the back door, then stopped dead in her tracks, turned around and did a double take as she spotted the feathers on the lawn. I could almost hear her thinking 'what has happened here?' as she started sniffing the feathers and looked at me again.

We all went outside and I held the pigeon out to her. 'Look what I have for you darling - a special present' I said. She backed off and looked at me suspiciously, as if she could not believe her eyes. I suppose she was expecting it to fly away any minute. She turned her face away from me and looked away.

'Come on then girl, it is for you, come and get it', I encouraged her, waving the bird in front of her. She hesitated and sniffed the air, about six feet away from me. Then, before I could blink, she snatched it away from me and ran.

My friend just managed to get her tail in the picture as she disappeared under the gate with her treasure - so much for my photo. 'Oh well, we shall not see her again tonight', said my friend. However, within five minutes, Foxyloxy was back for her dinner, and we burst out laughing - we could not believe it. She must have given the pigeon to her cubs. We all gave her a piece of chicken and she took the rest home. My foxy family must have had a right royal feast that night.

Talking about a feast, one day I was at a lunch for a special occasion. There were about one hundred guests seated at tables for ten. For the main course, an entire enormous roast turkey graced each table, for us to help ourselves. It was delicious and great fun, but at the end of the meal, there was a great deal of the turkey left over. 'Turkey sandwiches next week', I remarked as the waiter cleared the table. 'Oh no madam', he said. 'Turkey curry?' I suggested. He shook his head.

I asked the waiter what they were going to do with it then. 'It will have to be thrown away, madam' he said. 'As it's been on the table, we cannot use it again'.

Some people at the other tables asked for a doggy bag. Great idea, I thought. When it came to feeding Foxyloxy, I had no pride left. However, I did get some very odd looks as I asked if I could have a doggy bag for my fox. Well, I did not want people to think I was that desperate for myself!

The chef wrapped half a turkey in foil for me and it fed my fox family for three days. I never even had a turkey sandwich. Happy Christmas, Foxyloxy!

CHAPTER FOURTEEN

A nasty incident

Emma and Marcus came back at the end of July; they were going to stay for the entire six weeks of the school holiday and we had planned a road trip to Holland during the third week of August. They were always pleased to see my fox and helped to feed her again. It is a good thing we all love chicken for dinner, as I must have bought dozens over the months when Foxyloxy was around so we could share them. Yes, she was a very entertaining fox, if an expensive one.

It was not just all the food she ate either. I came home from a walk with Emma and Marcus one afternoon and Emma left her muddy sandals outside the door. 'Don't leave them there', I said, 'Foxyloxy will have those'. We went in to take our coats off and hung them in the hall. Not ten minutes later one of the sandals was on the grass with the strap chewed in half.

She managed to chew the handle off another bag too - do not ask me how, we never saw her do it. Oh, and then there was the day one of the men in the road lost one of his work boots from his doorstep, and it was found a couple of days later, several gardens along the road. He told me about it and I warned him about her thieving habits, but he ignored me so she promptly did it again a week later. This time, he did not find his boot again. She must have taken it for her cubs to play with. What a naughty girl! Cubs like to play and to chew things; shoes, gardening gloves and balls act as teething rings and exercise their jaw muscles. Dogs are the same, as anyone who has ever owned a puppy will testify.

Several feeding dishes disappeared from the lawn as well; they were only plastic, but even so. I did find a couple, one in a neighbour's garden and one down the lane. Clearly, Foxy and family had a take-away!

One night, I heard more fox noise than normally and when I looked out, I saw to my bewilderment that Foxyloxy was screaming at one of her cubs as she chased it down the road. Furthermore, every time it tried to come back and join the other two for some food, they turned on it as well and would not let it get near the bowl. It was upsetting for me to see this young fox trying to get back to its mum and siblings, but the rest of the family did not want this youngster with them any longer and that was it. I wondered if this one was the timid shy cub, poor little thing.

Because the little cub kept trying to come back, the arguments carried on several more nights, waking me and my immediate neighbours on more than one occasion. I did not have to go to work the next day as I am retired, but the neighbours who did were, understandably, not impressed with the nightly goings-on in the road and in my garden.

To lessen the disturbance, whenever I heard the cubs making a noise on the lawn, I used to get up and 'shush' them or clap my hands, which usually worked fine. The little foxes were wary and fearful; their instinct told them to keep away from people. Even their mother was the same with unexpected noises, despite her friendliness towards me. Just opening the squeaky bedroom window was often enough to send them all scampering away. All but Foxyloxy of course. She would take a few paces, look at me in disgust as if to say 'why did you scare my babies away?' and then carry on feeding quietly.

On one of these occasions, at 3 am, the cubs were on the lawn squabbling noisily and Foxyloxy was looking at them from the path. I was watching them fight when I heard a front door open, two doors away from my house. I heard a whispered command and next thing I knew a big Staffordshire bull terrier-type dog rushed out and charged after the cubs. They ran for their lives, including Foxyloxy, as he stormed down the road after them. I held my breath in alarm; I was sure he was going to catch one of them. I waited for the inevitable screams as he caught and massacred one. However, nothing happened and a minute or so later, I heard the owner call the dog back, it ran home and he slammed the door shut. Phew, what a relief, they had all escaped the dog.

I did not sleep another wink after that. Foxyloxy and her cubs were safe for the moment, but I was shaking with nerves and anxiety at what I had witnessed, I feared for the safety of my foxy family; I was also outraged that this man had purposely set his dog on them, as I was certain that this was unlawful. I felt sick and I lay there, trembling, thinking of how to deal with the situation. I was not keen to confront him myself as he intimidates me; on the other hand, I could not ignore this episode. The cubs and their mother must have been terrified. How cruel.

While watching the cubs in my garden, I had often seen this man walk his dog just before midnight. The dog was never on a lead and sometimes the owner even let it out on its own to do its business before bedtime. However, this incident had taken place at 3 am; it was obvious he was annoyed at the foxes' noises. They must have woken him up, just as they had me. I decided that I would ask for advice from the police as to the legality of setting a dog on fox cubs. I wanted to be sure of the facts.

Emma and Marcus slept through the whole event and were horrified to learn what had happened in the night. The idea of going to the police station was exciting for them, and off we went. I explained to the police officer at the desk what had happened and told him how worried we were. He told us that it was definitely 'not OK' to set a dog on fox cubs, however, the police would not get involved in this; he advised us to speak to the RSPCA. The same morning, we went to the local RSPCA to explain my predicament and worries again. They also said that it was illegal to chase foxes and cubs with a dog, and advised us to phone their emergency number.

Once home again, I phoned the RSPCA emergency number as advised; the person answering the phone was very short with me.

'Has a fox been killed?' she asked me after I told her what had happened.

'No, but it would have been had the dog got hold of one' I said.

'Did you see the person and did you hear what command was given?'

'No, I cannot see them, they are close by on the same side of the street as me and the command was whispered, not shouted out so I don't know what he said, besides it was the middle of the night, 3 am, and it was pitch black'.

'Oh, well, it's not an emergency then' she replied.

'Oh yes, it is to me, what if it happens again? Are you telling me that you are not interested until that dog kills one of the cubs? I thought you were there for the prevention of cruelty to animals, can you not go and have a word with that man?' I pleaded.

'No, it is not an emergency and we are busy with real emergencies, so goodbye!' and she put the phone down. I was livid! How could they not care? Was this not cruelty to animals? I thought they were there to prevent that. I was not impressed. Maybe they are only there for domestic animals, and not wildlife, but it was my local RSPCA branch who had told me to phone them in the first place.

I was particularly worried because we were going to Holland soon; I would be away for about nine days and would be unable to keep an eye on my beloved Foxyloxy and her family, so to me this situation was an emergency and I wanted somebody with authority to go and have a word with the owner of the dog in order to prevent a possible repeat performance resulting in the death of a cub or even worse, of Foxyloxy herself. It didn't bear thinking about.

I phoned the local council and asked to speak to the dog warden, but he was not in his office and I would have to wait a couple of days as he was out the next day as well. What could I do now? I was facing another couple of nights of possible disturbance and a potential repeat threat from the dog. I decided I would email the dog warden so that he would have my message as soon as possible.

I watched out for my foxy family during the next two nights and saw my neighbour walking his dog again – off the lead as usual. Fortunately, the foxes behaved quite well those two nights, although I did not sleep much with the stress of it all. The next night saw Foxyloxy chase her third cub away again amid some noise. It was only 1 am and yet again, the dog came rushing out of the house on command, same as before. He gave chase but failed again to catch a cub, which was very fortunate. The foxes had managed to outrun the dog for the second time. I was beside myself; how long could this go on?

In the morning, I had an email back from the dog warden with a request to telephone him. I did that and explained the worrying situation; he said he would 'have a word'. From him I learnt that it is not even legal to walk a dog off lead in a residential area and that it is certainly not all right to encourage it to chase after fox cubs, as I already knew.

My friend further along the road told me she had also been worried about that dog. She lives on the other side of the owner and her cats had become increasingly nervous, scared even, to approach their house and refused to come in at night when the dog was loose in the road. I exchanged a couple more emails and phone calls with the dog warden, explaining that I did not leave food out all night and that the overflowing bins in the front garden of the dog owner were more likely to attract vermin than the few peanuts left in my garden after the foxes had polished off the chicken and sausages. Those never lasted for more than 10 minutes. He agreed with me and said it was not against the law to feed the foxes. I also mentioned that I liked looking out for the foxes, to make sure they were all right and told him what

I had learned about the lives of foxes, thanks to Professor Stephen Harris' book; I emailed him a photo of Foxyloxy, which he liked; he printed it and put it on the notice board in his office.

He must have spoken to the dog owners, because the next night, while watching my foxes as normal, I noticed the man and his dog – off the lead - coming home from a walk. I heard him talk and a second later, his wife came out of the house and started shouting at me and accusing me, among other things, of 'spying on them and grassing them up to the council'. I did think the fact that she had used the words 'grassing' implied some guilt on their part; however I did not reply, as I am not in the habit of yelling insults at my neighbours, least of all out of a window in the middle of the night.

The dog owner took no notice of the dog warden's warning though and continued to walk his dog off lead at night; he was obviously above the law. I did not trust him at all. However, I saw no more chases in the night, which was just as well as I was just about a nervous wreck by now.

Foxyloxy and her cubs were still coming to eat about 11pm. They were also about later in the night and she and her two bigger cubs were still arguing with the third cub, who continued to try to come near to eat. I suppose he did not understand that it was time for him to go and find his own territory. I did feel sorry for him and nature is nature, but it did seem very harsh at the time.

Shortly after all this, the children and I went away on holiday. Jenny fed the animals as usual and, as I did not receive any texts from her to the contrary, I assumed everything at home was all right. Mine is a corner house so, before I went away, I had started to feed the foxes at the side of the house in order to minimise the noises in the front, which Jenny continued to do as well.

When we returned home at the beginning of the last week of August, we were absolutely delighted to see Foxyloxy come down the road when we called her. She was beginning to look like her old self, with a new coat growing in and her tail looking thicker as well. The two cubs I had seen in the night seemed to have grown as well and were almost bigger than she was. It was difficult to tell the difference now.

Hold on, two cubs? Yes, there were just two cubs now. Evidently, Foxyloxy had managed to get rid of her third cub while I was away. Poor little thing, I wondered what would become of it.

It was easy to tell the remaining cubs apart: one did not have a white tip to the tail and was greyer all over, while the other had the typical white-tipped red brush. They were both little vixens and Emma suggested we called them 'Mori' and 'Rose' respectively, after the supermarkets where we bought all their food, Morrison and Waitrose! I thought that was hilarious, it was a great idea and the names stuck.

CHAPTER FIFTEEN

Where is Foxyloxy?

We had another lovely week. Foxyloxy came during the day and did all her usual things, posing and sleeping on the lawn and mooching around in the front and the back garden at various times. One evening, I had to look twice when I saw her asleep on the lawn; she looked so tiny that I thought she was one of the cubs.

As I sat in the grass next to her, she did not move, did not even sit up. She looked so small and vulnerable and a bit sad, which made me wonder if she was all right. I had to use all my willpower not to stroke her; she looked as if she needed comforting. She was fine the day after that. I had worried for nothing again, maybe she had just had an 'off' day.

Emma, Marcus and I fed her at the back door or the front door depending on where she happened to turn up when we called her in the evening. I saw her with her cubs in the night and we all talked to her and continued to take her pictures for the rest of the week.

On the last day of August, we went to the cinema in the

afternoon and when we came back around 7 pm Foxyloxy was sitting at the end of the road near where the lane begins and was looking at us. We called to her as we went inside to get her food, expecting her to come, but she did not appear in the back garden, or the front. When I went back outside to see where she was, she was still sitting there on the path near the lane, and she needed quite a bit of persuasion and calling before she came to us. The children were waving a drumstick at her and calling her to come, but she seemed really hesitant before she finally did come over to eat it. She did not take any food away with her either; I could not understand it. During the night, Rose and Mori came and finished all the food. Mum was not with them and they ate quite peacefully together now there were just two of them.

Foxyloxy did not appear the next three nights and Emma and Marcus went home at the end of the week without seeing her again. After they went home, I called Foxyloxy several times during the evenings and started to look for her down the lane as well, calling for her, but she did not come. Just her two girls were here in the night. After ten days, I was extremely worried and wondering what had happened to stop her coming to me.

Emma and Marcus asked after her, and friends who knew she had not been to see me asked after her. They made comments such as 'oh, she'll be back', 'she may have gone back to the wild', 'her big cubs might have chased her off her territory' and even 'maybe she has been killed'.

I was getting distressed; it was now over two weeks since I had last seen her, the longest she had ever been away. I asked the Fox Project where she could be and whether a wounded fox from my area had been admitted perhaps. She would be easy to identify because of the scar on her left leg. They said that vixens sometimes leave their territory when their cubs are big. I found it hard to believe she would leave such a good food source and her family. Truth be told, I found it hard to believe she would leave me; how arrogant can you get? The answer is very, apparently.

During the next fortnight, in desperation, I walked through the nearby common at dusk. I also walked down the lane two, three times a day carrying some food and calling her name. It was no use; on the common, by the lakes and along the stream, I could not really see any place for her to hide, and I had no luck in the lane either. She just was not there. In any case, I was convinced that if she had heard me calling she would have come to me. She had been my regular visitor for 17 months from when she first came in the dark with her mother and sibling, then sitting abandoned on the lawn, to becoming my special friend. She had made me learn all about her species and educated and entertained my family and friends, and I had grown to love her like a pet. By now, I had at least 400 photographs of her and her cubs, and Rose and Mori were still here every night.

I started getting an awful sense of foreboding and sadness. Would she ever come back? Why would she leave her family or her territory, or me for that matter? I did not understand, believe or accept that she had just gone away. It was like losing a beloved pet. Not knowing what had happened to her was the worst of it all.

The sad truth is, however, that I never did see her again. I felt bereaved; I could not look at her photographs without tears, and I still find it hard not to think of her when I am sitting in the garden. I visualise her sitting on the table and lying in my chair and I remember every little thing she did. In fact, as I write this chapter tears are falling on the keyboard. It brings back the pain of loss in those first weeks without her. I had looked out for her, fed her, treated her when she was hurt, worried about her and her cubs, and I felt completely helpless now. She had made me laugh a lot when she was here and now she made me cry by not being there. In my dreams at night, I saw her at the door and felt happy because she was back. On waking to find it was only a dream, I felt miserable and upset. I could not talk about her without getting tearful. My Nature Watch friends understood and gave their support, but while I appreciated their friendship, and still do, it did not lessen my pain. What had she done to me? What had I done to myself, letting her get so close?

She was such a special friend, particularly as she was a wild animal whose trust I had gained. Beautiful and gentle, she had walked right into my heart, treading all over it; she broke it with her disappearance and left only the fang marks in my purse and her two grown up cubs.

I will never forget my fabulous, glorious, wild girl, Foxyloxy.

CHAPTER SIXTEEN

The final chapter

One consolation has been the fact that Foxyloxy's two daughters Rose and Mori are still here nearly a year later, and that Rose gave birth to five cubs in March. Rose is the vixen with the white-tipped tail. She only comes in the night with her cubs. Sometimes her sister, Mori, is with her and sometimes her mate, who I've called 'Prince'. He must be the father of the cubs, since she tolerates him near her and them. She looks wonderful and is bigger than he is, which is unusual in the foxy world.

I still feed all of them every night, and watching the cubs grow has been a delight. They are completely wild and scarper as soon as they see or hear me. I spy on them and watch Rose sit in the middle of the street with all her cubs around her, just as her mother used to do. They follow her around and fight over food among themselves. Occasionally, she has only two or three cubs with her and I see Prince with the others.

As before in her family, there is one dominant cub and

one timid cub with the rest somewhere in between; I cannot tell them apart in the dark but I can see three have a white-tipped tail and two have a completely grey tail. I still get a great deal of enjoyment out of fox watching, the cubs are so funny. The other night, the dominant cub sat in the food dish and did not let anyone else near – not even his mother, what a cheek!

Some nights I see the whole family eat together, while at other times Rose and the other adults take food away to the cubs and I can hear them arguing. Rose just jumps over the fence when I call her by rattling the peanuts and dog biscuits in the dish and clicking my tongue. They still seem to be in a garden opposite my house, behind the fencing, where Foxyloxy was with her cubs. Prince appears to live down the lane, as he always comes from that direction. Rose watches and waits for him to approach from there before coming over. They greet each other by licking and nibbling each other's ears. It is obvious to me that they are a pair.

When Rose first came with them, the cubs hid in the hedge opposite, since they were too small yet to jump a six-foot fence. They squeezed through a hole to go into the Close, where they hid under cars and bushes; from there they moved into my front garden. Rose normally told them when it was safe to come over and I could hear excited yapping. They must have smelled the chicken and other foods; they did not need telling twice, and were usually here within seconds, keeping to the shadows of the parked cars. The braver ones ran straight across the road.

From a distance, Rose looks just like her mother and is just as caring. She knows me and comes nearer than any other family members will, but she only comes in the dark and no closer than about 20 feet from me. Therefore, I have no clear pictures of her and the cubs, only grainy ones, taken out of the bedroom window. I continue to worry about my foxy family, as recently Rose has been limping – she must have landed awkwardly after jumping those fences.

Her mate is also a bit of a wounded prince. He seems unable to jump the fences and always walks the long way around to get to the cubs. I think a dog down the lane caught him one evening when the cubs were very young. I heard terrible squealing, barking and growling, followed by a frantic scrabbling up a fence.

Following that incident, I saw him again on several occasions. At first, he was dragging his entire back body along; he could not stand on his back legs at all. I was horrified as the lower half of his body appeared paralysed. With his front legs he pulled himself along little by little through the bushes of four other gardens to reach mine, while Rose or Mori walked slowly along the path with him; they were always there and watched over him while he fed. They walked back with him too and returned later to feed themselves and take food away for the cubs. It was pitiful to see him and I wondered what I could do to help him. Some days I did not see him at all and Rose and her sister just took food away. They were more caring than some people I know; it was extremely moving to observe the family dynamics.

Cage-trapping him for possible treatment had not been an option, as there were so many adults and cubs around at that time. If we had caught the wrong fox, they might all have stopped coming. Having to find a new territory would have put all the adults and cubs at risk, as other foxes would not have tolerated them on their patch in the neighbourhood.

I was delighted when he slowly improved and managed to wobble and limp his way here again on his own. He ate while sitting up, but he was still very unsteady and looked as if he was going to fall over any minute. There was a large, bare scar visible on his back about eight inches from the base of his tail and his right hind foot had a raw wound, causing his limp. He must have been in agony.

When I consulted my book, I learnt that a fox with a lower back injury could recover well, which gave me hope. Indeed, against all the odds, he has recovered slowly; limping badly at first but after another three months, walking normally again, although he no longer jumps the fences. The scar has healed, with new dark fur growing on it, and he has helped to rear the cubs like a good dad. Two of the cubs always seemed to be with him while Rose had the other three.

It is September 2013 now, and sometimes I find it difficult to see who is who. The three cubs that are still here are practically fully-grown – they are slightly smaller, sleeker versions of their beautiful mother. They are very wary and always run away when they spot me watching them, probably just as well. Rose will come when called, but she waits until I have gone back in the house and have closed the door before she comes on to the lawn to feed. I do talk to her, but she will not come close. I tell her she is not like her mother, despite the fact that she looks just like her. Recently she has taken to sitting on top of my car and staring at my house. She reminds me of her mother Foxyloxy, who used to sit on the garden table and stare in through the patio doors.

Sometimes I see Rose again before going to bed and she

just looks at me. I usually come back downstairs and give her an egg, because she always lets the cubs eat most of the food. I am sure she knows this and will sit or lie on the path outside the house until all the lights are out again. I have even called her 'Foxyloxy' thinking it might have been her. She did not react; it was not her.

I have not seen Mori for several weeks; perhaps her role as a helper and babysitter has ended now that the cubs are big and can forage for themselves. I hope she is safe and well - Foxyloxy's other daughter.

It will soon be time for this year's cubs, Rose's, to disperse. This generally happens in October and I wonder who is going to stay this time and where the other foxes will find a home. I hope they will be welcome wherever they go. Foxes are very capable and adaptable, so even if people do not feed them, they are so tender among themselves and so much fun to watch. Just don't let them walk into your heart.

Recently, I have discovered that my neighbour set his dog onto my foxes again while I was on holiday in August last year. As the family gave their dog away last autumn, the chasing is not an issue this year. Nevertheless, I wonder whether it could have been a deciding factor in Foxyloxy's disappearance. Maybe she thought my house was no longer a safe place to come to. How very sad.

I do however prefer to believe the suggestion by one of my equally fox-mad friends: 'maybe Foxyloxy went away in order to secure the future for her daughters, leaving you to look after them and their offspring, which you do'.
Isn't that a lovely thought?

I do know that I miss her dreadfully and that one year on, looking at her beautiful photos still distresses me. Like people, wild animals choose their friends. These friends are not always of the same species and occasionally they are human. Thank you for choosing me to be your friend, Foxyloxy. It has been an amazing journey.

More about foxes

If you have enjoyed the story of Foxyloxy and would like to know more about foxes in general, the National Fox Welfare Society has kindly helped me to compile the following information.

Red Fox *(Vulpes vulpes)*

The red fox is the largest member of the *Vulpes* genus (true foxes), of which there are 12 species across the world. It is characterised by the large bushy tail, often tipped with a white splash. Although commonly known as the red fox, many colour variations exist. The most common is rust red to flame red. The backs of the ears are black and the lower leg parts, often known as the socks, are typically black. Due to its hunting abilities and its elliptical eyes, some people imagine it to be part dog, part cat.

A female fox is called a vixen.

A male fox is called a dog fox.

A baby fox is called a cub or kit.

A group of foxes is called a skulk.

The place where cubs are born is known
as an earth or den.

The word 'fox' is derived from an ancient
Proto-Indo-European word meaning 'tail'.

Vital statistics

Total Length (cm): dog 67, vixen 63

Tail length (cm): dog 45, vixen 38

Weight (Kg): dog 6.7 vixen 5.4

Lifespan: Approximately 2 years in the wild and
up to 12 - 14 years in captivity

Gestation: Approximately 51-53 days

Litter Size: 4-5

Protection and legislation: In the UK there are no laws
specifically to protect foxes apart from the Wild Mammals Acts.

Distribution

The red fox is found throughout the Northern Hemisphere
from the Arctic Circle to North Africa, Central America
and the Asiatic Steppes, excluding Iceland, the Arctic

Islands and some parts of Siberia and the extreme desert. The red fox was also introduced to Australia and into the Eastern States of North America.

Habitat

Since the fox is so adaptable to its surroundings, the habitat requirements vary extremely, ie from Arctic tundra to busy city centres. Natural habitat is of a mixed landscape with abundant woodlands. The red fox can also be found thriving in deserts and upland mountains. The urban fox is flourishing and seems to be able to thrive when its territory is so closely associated with man.

Food

As with its requirements for habitat, foxes are very adaptable when it comes to diet, eating small mammals, beetles, earthworms, birds, garbage and carrion. The aspect of the fox's diet that surprises many is their love of fruit. When blackberries are ripe on the bushes, foxes will go blackberry picking and during this season, because of the fruit consumed, their droppings are often purple in colour.

Like any successful predator, a fox will leave nothing to waste. If food is abundant, the fox will cache its food for a day when there may be a shortage. One experiment carried out by zoologists in a gull colony where foxes regularly preyed on both birds and eggs found that the foxes would bury eggs in the sand dunes in the nesting season, when they were plentiful, and return months later to dig them up, finding them not by memory but by scent (*Nature Detective*, Hugh Falkus).

Many think, especially when the fox and chicken coop scenario is brought up, that foxes kill for fun. This is opportunism, not fun. A fox will kill all the chickens if it is able and try to cache what it can't eat for a later day.

The fox is known for its characteristic cat-like pounce on small rodents. On seeing this, one may ask why they expend so much energy by pouncing when to run up to the rodent would be less like hard work. The answer is simple - when a vole, for instance, is in danger from a fox it will leap into the air to avoid capture. The fox obviously anticipates this by coming down from above.

Behaviour

The fox is a very social animal and is usually territorial. Depending on the size of the territory and food availability, anything up to seven adults can form the family group. A strict hierarchy will be present where usually only the dominant animals will breed. The family will usually be made up of the dominant dog fox, dominant vixen, and several female helpers from previous litters. A certain number of cubs born in one year will disperse to find territories and mates of their own. Males tend to disperse further than females.

Foxes are usually active at dusk and dawn, but in quiet areas can be just as active during the day as in the night. More daytime activity increases as the mating season approaches. Both the dog fox and the vixen will only have a short amount of time in which they will be able to mate, so the dog fox will mirror every move of the vixen to ensure he will be there when the time is right. Although foxes mainly live above ground, the vixen, in January, will usually start preparing an earth in preparation for when she gives birth. The cubs are usually born in March and until they are 10-12 days old, the vixen will rarely leave their side. Not only will the cubs, up to this age, be unable to regulate their own heat, they will also be blind and deaf.

Cubs will usually be observed above ground in mid-April. If anything is wrong with one of her cubs the vixen will take it to a far corner of her territory and dump it. This behaviour ensures the remaining littermates do not become infected with something the cub may be carrying. After about three weeks, the vixen will start to lie away from her cubs to wean them off her milk onto solid foods. This food will usually be offered to the cubs through regurgitation for the first week or so. The young are completely independent by seven months and are able to breed when ten months of age.

Conservation

Because of the wide distribution of foxes, no conservation measures are needed for the species as a whole. Several organisations exist to look after injured or sick individual foxes. The fox is blamed across the world for taking livestock and this will always bring the fox into conflict with man. Foxes are trapped in high numbers for their fur. They are also killed in enormous numbers during rabies control schemes. However, following such control measures foxes usually rapidly recover their numbers; because of this the current approach involves using an oral vaccine. This has proven to have a very high success rate in many European countries.

The fox's year

January

January is usually a month of unrest within the fox family - not only is it the peak of the mating season, it is also the peak dispersal season. Cubs that were born last year, now adults, will be seen as a threat to the breeding rights and the available food supply of their parents. Any sub-adults who have failed to disperse will usually be continually chased away. Many of the sub-adults will actually leave of their own accord in search of a territory and a mate of their own. The resident dog fox and vixen will be actively defending the territory against intruders, both physically and vocally. They do this by barking, urinating and defecating along the borders of their territory.

Since it is the breeding season, the dog fox will shadow every move of the vixen; she is only receptive for a period of about three days. From the dog fox's point of view, he must ensure he is there when she is ready. Several attempts to mount the vixen will be rebuffed, sometimes quite aggressively. However, when she is ready, she flirts around the dog fox. Caution at this stage is thrown to the wind, and many people will observe the foxes in the process of mating.

When the vixen is ready the dog fox will grasp her from behind with his front two legs and start to mate. At this point the dog fox's penis is not totally erect until he has actually entered the vagina, when it becomes completely erect and the base of it begins to swell. Also, the vixen's vagina will constrict. This swelling and constriction will cause the pair to lock together, commonly called the 'tie'. When the dog fox ejaculates, he attempts to dismount, but as they are still locked together he brings one of his back legs over the vixen's back and there they stand, back to back, for the duration of the tie, possibly for hours.

Through instinct the vixen will start to prepare an earth prior to giving birth; in a town environment it's likely the chosen place will be under a garden shed. In the countryside, disused rabbit warrens are common, as are badger setts.

February

Quite the opposite of January, February is usually a relatively stable month for the fox family. The dispersal season is over and the fights over who breeds with whom have now stopped. While many of the litters born over the years disperse when old enough, some of the foxes, usually the females, may be allowed to stay on within their parents' territory. Although they will have given up their right to breed, some of the benefits outweigh this, i.e. a secure territory, a regular supply of food and knowledge of the area.

The dominant vixen is usually the only vixen allowed to mate, but females from previous litters will play their part in actually looking after and rearing the young when they are born. They act as aunties looking after the cubs while the vixen is away hunting, and will also bring food back for the cubs. In February, the vixen, during the day, will be denned down in the earth she has prepared.

March

The vixen will be confined to her earth at one point during this season because March is the peak cubbing season. If you are lucky enough to have witnessed the mating, by counting down between 51-53 days you will have an accurate idea as to when the cubs will be born.

The average litter of cubs is usually five in number, and when born they are blind and deaf. Being unable to regulate their own body heat, the vixen will not usually leave their side for about 10-11 days. At birth, the cubs weigh approximately 100 grams, and in addition to not being able to regulate their own heat, they rely solely on the vixen to stimulate them to urinate and defecate. Being denned down, the vixen relies on her dog fox to bring food - and heaven help him if he is late! If food has not been brought, the vixen will go to the mouth of the earth and give out several contact calls. Like many males of different species, the dog fox will at this time look like he has got the world on his shoulders and appears very lethargic.

It is usually March/April when householders report losses of pet rabbits and guinea pigs - as these are usually taken as an easy option for the dog fox with so many mouths to feed. The easiest option for ensuring you do not lose a pet rabbit or guinea pig in any month is to ensure you have provided adequate housing for them.

April

It will usually be a nice warm day in April when the cubs venture for the first time above ground. After a great play, they will often slump down in a pile and go to sleep out in the open. Play is an important role in any youngster's upbringing and it is during this play that mini pecking orders will start already to be established.

The vixen will still be kennelled down with them but now she will hunt for herself. The dog fox will usually lie close to the earth protecting the cubs from any unwanted attention from cats.

In March and April telephone calls from concerned householders peak, with people thinking that foxes are looking to kill cats to feed to the cubs. However, what is actually happening is that the cats which are attracted to the earth because of the noises of the cubs, are seen off by either the dog fox or vixen, in some cases both. Left to their own devices, when cubs are very young, cats will kill them as they would a bird.

May

To wean the cubs off her milk the vixen will lie away from them during the day, bringing small items of food back for them often. This behaviour leads many people to believe that cubs out on their own during the day, with no adult apparently around, must have been abandoned. To ensure this is not the case a good idea is to put down an egg about five feet from the earth. Cubs at this age will not be able to pick it up and move it, and the fox is really the only animal apart from badgers that will actually take the egg away. In short, if the egg has gone it means there is a fair chance an adult has visited the cubs. In contrast to puppies, fox cubs usually play silently to avoid attracting the attention of predators.

June

June is possibly the best month of the year to observe fox cubs at play, and it is usually in this month that the vixen will leave them in an area while she goes out hunting. This area, known as the play area, will also be where the vixen now starts bringing food to the cubs. It may also be to wean them from the earth, because later in the month, this will be abandoned and the cubs, like the adults, will lie above ground. Although still playing during the day, the cubs start to become more lethargic. Now completely weaned off their mother's milk, it will be the food she supplies that the cubs are reliant upon.

July

The cubs are becoming more self-sufficient, which may be due to the fact that the adults will bring back less food. Both dog fox and vixen will take the cubs out to known feeding sites, usually the cubs will be split e.g. 3 with the dog fox 2 with the vixen. How do they learn anything one wonders, when still all of their time is taken up playing.

August

Looking more like adults now, the cubs will start their

activities around the same time as the adults, most active between dusk and dawn. The latter half of the month gives a clue as to what they are all eating, adults included, as their droppings will be almost purple with the amount of blackberries picked. Fruit plays an important part in the fox's natural diet.

Cubs hunting for voles, mice etc. can be observed early in the morning perfecting the 'mouse pounce'. Cubs, after an initial play in the play area, will usually depart in two's for a night's foraging. At any point, if the vixen or dog fox detects danger, they will give out a sharp bark, which will send the cubs scurrying for cover. When in close proximity to the cubs the warning bark is more of a muffled cough. So, for anyone who has sat watching cubs, only to see them all disappear when you have tried to muffle a cough, you will now know it was you who gave them the warning!

September

The fox cubs are now almost full-grown, and apparently indistinguishable from their parents, though a trained eye would be able to tell the difference. The signal that the family is beginning to break up can usually be heard and, if you are in the right place at the right time, can be observed.

Fruit will be still high on the foxes' diet and the sub-adults will now start to forage alone. It is in this month that the foxes become more vocal, which I believe could be for two reasons - they are in the process of dispersing while trying to maintain contact with parents and siblings, or the resident foxes are becoming more hostile to their own offspring.

October

More people see a fox for the first time in this month than in any other, suggesting maybe that this is the peak time for dispersal. Many of the foxes born this year will now die under the wheels of a car, or snared etc, for they are crossing unfamiliar terrain. As is the case in most months of the year, on warm wet nights the foxes will spend most of their time hunting earthworms.

November

Even this early the vixen will start to investigate potential earths in preparation for the new year. If possible she will use an existing excavation, often an abandoned badger sett; while foxes dig only when they have to, badgers are compulsive diggers and make new tunnels and chambers every year, creating a handy surplus for the foxes. Often she will select two to three earths and this, I feel, is done so that when the new cubs are born, if one earth is disturbed in any way she will move them to another. Although many aggressive encounters can be heard, it will still be possible to observe the young foxes playing. Foxes will start to forage in quiet areas from 6 pm onwards.

December

With the mating season approaching, foxes will now be actively defending their territories. The triple bark, often followed by a scream, can be heard frequently. It is this call that leads many to believe the foxes are killing cats. Often the police will be called out in the belief that someone is being attacked.

The territory borders are now showing increasing evidence of fox activity, and the musky smell of foxes is evident.

* * * * * * * * * * * * * *

References and useful contacts

Urban Foxes - second edition, by Stephen Harris and Phil Baker

www.wildlifeonline.me.uk contains everything you've always wanted to know about all different kinds of wildlife: photos, species profiles, news, wildlife articles, Q&A, links, and much more. Includes a fantastic on-line monthly newsletter relevant to the natural world and wildlife of the month (by Marc Baldwin).

The Fox Project - www.foxproject.org.uk 01892 824111 A charity dedicated to the protection, rescue and advocacy for the wild fox. It offers advice, treatments and deterrents. Located in Tunbridge Wells, Kent. They operate a wildlife ambulance service within a 60 mile radius of their HQ between 9 am – 9pm. email: fox@foxproject.org.uk

Wildlife Hospital, Leatherhead - www.wildlifeaid.org.uk as seen on TV's 'Wildlife SOS'. 24hr emergency helpline: 09061 800 132

South Essex Wildlife Hospital –
www.southessexwildlife.org.uk 01375 893893
"Dedicated to putting 'life' back into the 'wild', this is a
wildlife rescue, rehabilitation and public advice charity,
caring for sick and injured wildlife and aiming to release it
back into the wild." Located in Thurrock, covering most
of Essex, East London and North Kent.

National Fox Welfare Society - www.nfws.org.uk 01933
411996

"NFWS leads the way forward in eliminating sarcoptic
mange/canine mange in foxes across the UK."
Sarcoptic mange/canine mange/fox mange is a terrible
condition which if left untreated will bring the death of
the infected fox. The NFWS believes that if a condition
can be treated then it should be, regardless of whether the
householder is unwilling, or unable to pay for the
treatment. If you have seen a fox with mange and would
be willing to provide food (in the form of a jam or honey
sandwiches each night), the treatment can be sent to you
free of charge. To receive mange treatment and an
information leaflet, please click on the sarcoptic mange
treatment link on their website.

'Stop Fox Hunting' on Facebook. Contains many stunning
fox photos. Full admin in place, so threats and abuse will
not be tolerated.

In May this year (2013), a film crew from Landmark Films
came to my house to film my new foxy family. This was for

a documentary on BBC1 about urban foxes, *Fox Wars* (see photo). It was shown on TV in October 2013. The foxes put on a sterling performance. They must have known they were on camera. Rose, Mori and Prince were all on the lawn, with the cubs running about all over the place. It was the first time I realised there were five cubs! I didn't get to see them on TV as the footage was too dark to use, but I was there in my kitchen preparing a foxy feast! Never mind, it was a very exciting evening.